CORPORATE INTERIORS

No.4

CORPORATE INTERIORS

No.4

Edited by
Roger Yee

Visual Reference Publications Inc., New York

Copyright © 2001 by Visual Reference Publications Inc.

Visual Reference Publications Inc.
302 Fifth Avenue
New York, NY 10001

Distributors to the trade in the United States and Canada
Watson-Guptill
770 Broadway
New York, NY 10003

Distributors outside the United States and Canada
HarperCollins International
10 East 53rd Street
New York, NY 10022-5299

Library of Congress Cataloging in Publication Data:
Corporate Interiors

Printed in Hong Kong
ISBN 1-58471-024-1

Book Design: Harish Patel Design Associates, New York

CONTENTS

Introduction   What is Corporate America thinking?
Take a look at where it works.

This is the fourth annual volume of a book that was conceived to answer three critical questions: What does Corporate America look like? Who makes it look that way? Why does it look that way? While there is an overabundance of books and magazines that show all types of residential design, there has not been—until this book appeared—an annual reference volume that can provide a timely, diverse and far-reaching overview of the latest developments in the design of corporate workplaces.

Corporate executives know why this book is needed as soon as they discover that there is a significant gap between the needs of their businesses and the capabilities of their facilities. Since most executives have little or no experience in developing buildings or interiors of buildings, not to mention entire corporate campuses, they suddenly face daunting tasks. What architect or interior designer should they choose to provide impartial advice on their options? Who are the best designs firms, where can they be found and what kind of work do they do?

The 64 top firms invited to participate in this book show examples of their work that are not only visually striking, they encompass a wide range of problem solving. In the pages that follow, you will share their thoughtful analyses and creative solutions to Corporate America's changing needs for affordable real estate, efficient space utilization, adequate power, voice and data services, and manageable workplace environments supported by good lighting, acoustics, air quality and ergonomic provisions.

If you have seen any of the previous volumes of this book, you will notice how much has changed in four years. Our case studies chart the explosion in information technology and worker productivity as well as the rise and fall of Internet-related companies, confirming a recent study commissioned by Knoll Inc. from the market research firm DYG Inc. In effect, Knoll's research proclaims that the office is not going away, that the best offices encourage employee innovation, productivity and self esteem, that the paperless office is pulp fiction, and that office status symbols mean less to workers than having the right office and tools for the job.

Beginning on page 540, you will find a perceptive essay about what it takes to develop a great office followed by information from companies making quality products you will want to discuss with your design team. In viewing the projects published here, you will probably find much to like. Just remember that you are surveying only a fraction of each firm's capabilities—and the corporate facility that is best for your business can only be determined by working with your architect or interior designer. As our pages show, many corporate executives have done just that—with superb results

Lester Dundes
Publisher

Ai

2100 M Street NW
Suite 800
Washington DC 20037
202.737.1020
202.223.1570 (Fax)
www.aiarchitecture.com
kreid@aiarchitecture.com   San Francisco

Ai

Left: *Auditorium.*
Below: *Conference center.*
Opposite: *Atrium.*
Photography: *Jeff Goldberg/Esto Photographics.*

How do you create a workplace to fulfill a client's business requirements—and surround its occupants in exciting architecture? This was America Online's objective in asking Ai to design its 230,000-square foot, four-story Creative Center 2 in Dulles, Virginia for 700 employees. The resulting facility, including private offices, conference center, auditorium, cafeteria and an 850-car parking structure, stands at the south end of a site whose master plan envisions 100 acres of development with over 2 million square feet of office space. It is organized internally by a primary circulation spine running north-south through the center of the building, linking two central cores spaced between three atria, and is furnished with a full-height furniture system and such basic materials as concrete, stainless steel, glass, maple wood and aluminum. What makes the environment come alive is its dynamic handling of forms and volumes, using angled walls, articulated ceilings, abundant windows, muted primary colors and dramatic lighting to celebrate a sophisticated modern view of life in sharp contrast to the wooded site outside the windows.

Right: Corridor.
Below left: Cafeteria.
Below right: Atrium skylight.

Ai

**The Rome Group
Washington, DC**

The Rome Group, a commercial real estate brokerage firm in Washington, D.C., faced a basic urban design problem that is commonly encountered by organizations locating in densely developed areas, namely that of bringing scarce daylight into a largely windowless space. To accomplish this and to impart a "loft like feel" to the 4,500-square foot office for 15 employees, Ai has created aluminum-framed storefronts glazed in structural polycarbonate panels to enclose volumes within an environment of private offices, open area work stations, conference room, workroom and lunchroom. These storefronts are in turn complemented by an architectural vocabulary of wood, metal, concrete, carpet, wire glass and floor paint, as well as a vibrant blue color applied to walls. Occupying a commanding position on the floor, the conference room acts like a lantern, radiating natural and man-made illumination to provide a cool, contemporary backdrop for the rest of the facility. A limited supply of daylight goes a long way here.

MCI WorldCom
Advanced Networks/UUNet
Reston, Virginia

Operations, marketing and training are vital to business, so MCI WorldCom was pleased to see how Ai developed a cost-effective and appealing 35,000-square foot environment on two floors of a speculative office building to house these activities. Ai created a set of architectural "objects" that appear as inserted forms and create spatial experiences in the residual spaces around them. Amid these accommodations is a much appreciated sectional garage door at the breakout area, because along with such materials as glass, stained concrete, carpet and tile there is room for fun.

Above: *Reception.*
Right: *Breakout area.*
Photography: *Walter Smalling, Jr.*

Shandwick Public Affairs
Washington, DC

You don't have to know about the plight of cartoonist Scott Adams's Dilbert to know how office workers feel about "cube farms." Determined to house its people in a supportive setting, Shandwick Public Affairs asked Ai to design a 25,000-square foot open plan environment with quality work stations and a multi-purpose zone near the entrance for reception, conference and entertaining. The custom work stations of wood, Plexiglas and perforated metal feel reassuringly open, and the multi-purpose zone's gathering places, featuring a cafe, have become favored places to meet, work and relax.

Above: *Conference room with pivot doors.*
Right: *Reception.*
Photography: *Walter Smalling, Jr.*

Ai

Interliant
Reston, Virginia

Above: *Reception desk.*
Photography: *Walter Smalling, Jr.*

An office space separated by a public lobby can be a liability. However, for Interliant, the distance between its marketing center and its high-security national operations center in a 25,000-square foot facility in Reston, Virginia, turned out to be ideal. In the design by Ai, each area shares similar architectural elements. However, color and animated signage let Ai divert visitors from the highly secured area while giving all employees a functional and attractive setting of wood, aluminum, terrazzo, carpet, perforated metal, glass and views of trees— unthinkable in the previous basement site.

Alan Gaynor + Company, P.C.

434 Broadway
New York
New York 10013
212.334.0900
212.966.8652 (Fax)
www.gaynordesign.com

Alan Gaynor + Company, P.C.

Intrasphere Technologies Inc.
New York, New York

A fascinating cultural dilemma in the high-technology world that remains unresolved is the need to create a formal setting for clients and investors, who tend to be middle-aged, methodical and reserved, that is also a desirable workplace for employees, who tend to be young, creative and informal. Intrasphere Technologies Inc., a developer of customized software in New York, had to deal with just this situation in its 16,000-square foot office for 62 employees designed by Alan Gaynor + Company, P.C. The company wanted to accommodate the two groups without clearly separating them. How do you do this in such varied facilities as reception, conference rooms, war rooms, open plan areas, private offices, server room, mailroom, lunchroom and breakout rooms? The answer lies in exploring the name, Intrasphere, with a design based on "entering a sphere." An environment of walls and work station clusters angled off the building grid, curving walls at transitional areas, and an imaginative lighting scheme has made the whole greater than the sum of its parts at Intrasphere.

Alan Gaynor + Company, P.C.

International Securities Exchange
New York, New York

Above: *Reception.*
Opposite: *Boardroom.*
Photography: *Roy Wright.*

One of the most creative financial marketplaces in the world, the United States recently saw the opening of its first electronic options exchange when the Securities Exchange Commission approved the birth of the International Securities Exchange. To house the ISE, Alan Gaynor + Company, P.C. has designed a 30,000-square foot, two-story facility for 75 people in lower Manhattan—just steps from the New York Stock Exchange—that includes private offices, open plan areas, conference and board rooms, data center, command center, war room, training room, pantry and interior staircase. Given the significance of the information technology driving ISE operations, its new office could almost be considered a computer with attendants, particularly since the data center alone occupies 20,000 square feet of space. However, the interior design skillfully creates a progressive image for the ISE that captures the high-technology "cutting edge" nature of the business as well as the solid business experience of the leadership-combining wood, fabric, leather and glass to establish first-class Wall Street credentials.

Alan Gaynor + Company, P.C.

Excite@Home
New York, New York

Above: Reception and interior staircase.
Below: Meeting room.
Opposite: Custom ceiling waffle and solar shade panels.
Photography: Roy Wright.

Though widespread commercial use of the Internet is not even 10 years old, a few Internet portals and Internet service providers (ISPs) have already emerged as the dominant forces in this new medium. One of the top contenders is Excite@Home, whose new, 30,000-square foot office in New York for 90 employees was designed by Alan Gaynor + Company, P.C. The basic description of the space may not indicate what makes it so distinctive. After all, who doesn't need its private offices, open plan areas, formal and informal meeting rooms, breakout areas, server room, office service areas, entertainment room, pantry and lunchroom? However, Excite@Home imposed three conditions that required fresh design ideas. First, the space had to maintain both perimeter offices and views of midtown Manhattan. Then, standard fluorescent lighting

was prohibited. Finally, the environment had to be playful as well as functional. To offer perimeter offices and views, glass partitions were installed as private office enclosures, along with one-foot wide vertical glass slots through interior partitions that aligned with exterior views. To illuminate the office, a waffle-patterned ceiling grid of cove fluorescent strips was installed that bounced light off a ceiling grid of solar shade material linking the entire space together. And to nurture a sense of play, open plan areas were arranged around central open breakout areas and divided from each other using whimsically shaped meeting spaces with funky variations on traditional lounge seating. The result could almost rival Excite@Home itself as an inviting destination.

Above: *View through partitions and ceiling grids.*
Left: *Interior staircase.*

AREA

550 South Hope Street
18th Floor
Los Angeles
California 90071
213.623.8909
213.623.4275 (Fax)
info@areaarchitecture.com

Bel Air Investment Advisors LLC
Los Angeles, California

No one investing for Barbra Streisand, Donna Karan and other high-profile individuals could fail to be influenced by them in establishing an office. Indeed, the clients set the tone for Bel Air Investment Advisors' first office years ago. Today, key players from Goldman Sachs who specialize in personal portfolio investment have joined with Bear Stearns as an underwriting partner to create a new Bel Air that can be visited in its new, 8,500-square foot Los Angeles office for 35 employees, designed by AREA. Having admired a New York investment company's workplace that was "mostly glass and centered around the trading desk," Bel Air now has its own glass pavilion with a twist: comfortable residential-style furnishings. Total openness is appropriate here, since trading is stimulated when traders can see and hear one another. On the other hand, glass walls and electronically operated shades are available for privacy. The finishing touches are provided by such upscale and environmentally responsible appointments as Persian rugs, cultivated wood veneers, French Art Deco lounge furniture and blue-chip art. Bel Air's discriminating clientele may look forward to elegant meetings where they may view the machinery of investment in action.

Above: Partner's office.
Below left: Open plan area and conference room.
Below right: Trading room.
Opposite: Conference room and reception at rear.
Photography: Jon Miller/Hedrich Blessing.

Julien J. Studley, Inc.
Los Angeles, California

Below: *Main conference room.*
Photography: *Jon Miller/Hedrich Blessing.*

Right: Reception looking at main conference
room.
Below left: Open plan
area.
Below right: Reception
looking at small confer-
ence room.

Few real estate broker-
ages would embrace an
art gallery aesthetic—or
have world-class art for
it. Yet because the Los
Angeles office of Julien
J. Studley, Inc. serves the
motion picture industry
capital and second
largest city in America,

the idea is not so out-
landish. In the design of
the 12,000-square foot
space for 45 employees,
AREA has met all stan-
dard functional require-
ments without creating a
standard facility. Ceilings,
for example, are
exposed, painted white

and accentuated with
soffits. An acoustical fabric ceiling hovers over
open plan work stations
to reflect light and pro-
vide sound privacy. A
sheet of glass converts a
work station from public
to private. Most lighting
is ambient, making the

track-lighted art the
focus of attention. Yes,
it's a real estate brokerage.

29

Klasky Csupo Animation Studio
Hollywood, California

Right: *Main conference room at reception entrance.*
Below: *Main reception.*
Opposite: *Pantry under a large ceiling form.*
Photography: *Jon Miller/Hedrich Blessing.*

What the Rugrats did to Paris in their recent, full-length feature film is not that different from what Klasky Csupo, the animator for the Rugrats, Ahh! Real Monsters and The Wild Thornberries, has done to a former Mercedes-Benz dealership on Hollywood's Sunset Boulevard. And why not? To consolidate all activities in a new headquarters, Klasky Csupo acquired the 100,000-square foot structure and retained AREA to transform it into an animation studio. The main floor area was vast—76,000 square feet—and the ceiling soared—25 feet—but considerable alternations were needed. Service bays, for instance, lacked windows or air conditioning and offered minimal electrical service, the vast floor area had to be reduced in scale to sustain any feeling of intimacy or identity, and the animator wanted to resist being "branded" by a slick workplace. AREA satisfied Klasky Csupo by exploiting the building's strengths. The ceiling accommodated the required air and

power units as well as an abstract landscape of shapes and forms that enclose rooms and make open areas feel like the dark, moody and mysterious neighborhoods animators like. Windows have been cut into the building's skin to admit natural light. Open plan work stations are built for convenience and reconfiguration with indirect lighting in splines and corners connected with bolted steel plates. This being a Rugrats' hangout, AREA has also planted some surprises: A "true to the architecture" aesthetic contrasts unfinished columns, ceilings and mechanical and electrical equipment with the colorful interior design, and a red ovoid entrance form crashes through a wall to announce the reception area. Voila— both animators and Rugrats appear to be delighted with their new home.

Above left: *Open area with large forms.*
Above right: *Another aspect of open area.*

Aref & Associates Design Studio

2221 Park Place
El Segundo
California 90245
310.426.7300
310.426.7310 (Fax)
www.aref.com
faaref@aref.com

Aref & Associates
Design Studio

The Boston Consulting Group
Los Angeles, California

Left: *Teaming office.*
Far left: *Secretarial work space.*
Below: *Conference room.*
Below: *Commons with cappuccino bar.*
Opposite: *Reception area.*
Photography: *Paul Bielenberg.*

One of the most prestigious global management consulting firms, is The Boston Consulting Group, whose new, 25,000-square foot facility designed by Aref & Associates for over 100 personnel in a 42-story, downtown Los Angeles office tower demonstrates how to provide effective, individualized accommodations for a bright, and highly skilled staff using functional, economical, and standardized offices. The innovative features include single-size offices that can change occupancy levels and accept modifications to serve officers, managers and consultants, plug-and-play wiring and multimedia capability, a multifunctional teamwork-oriented commons space and a staff lounge. In this dynamic commons space setting, a client's strategy or an impromptu round of backgammon with cappuccino can receive the attention they deserve.

34

Aref & Associates Design Studio

Troop, Steuber, Pasich, Reddick and Tobey, LLP
Los Angeles, California

Below: Reception area.
Photography: Paul Bielenberg.

Right: Main conference room.
Middle left: Conference room.
Lower left: Secretarial work stations.
Bottom left: Attorney office with teaming area.
Bottom right: Reception waiting area.

Don't ask today's attorneys where the law library is—because many of them neither know nor care. The impact of information technology is certainly legible at the 112,000-square foot law office of Troop, Steuber, Pasich, Reddick and Tobey, designed by Aref & Associates for up to 200 attorneys and a total workforce of 400 in a 44-story structure that is part of Century City Towers in Los Angeles. While a law compact library has been incorporated in the space, it is more significant that all private offices for attorneys and paralegals, conference rooms and case rooms, war room, imaging rooms and secretarial work stations are equipped with plug-and-play wiring that reflect the full acceptance of CD-ROMs and the Internet. The result is a superb venue for the practice of 21st century law.

Aref & Associates
Design Studio

Digital Media Campus
El Segundo, California

Above: Reception area.
Right: General office space.
Upper right: Kitchenette and copy center in suspended tent.
Below: Conference room with multi-media table.
Opposite: Plug-and-play conference room.
Photography: Paul Bielenberg.

Forget the headlines pitting dot-com mania versus dot-com phobia. Think about the profound impact of the "new economy" on the workplace environment. Whatever happens to businesses selling products to consumers and other businesses on the Web, the world is not likely to forget the spellbinding images from the late 1990s of bright, gifted and fiercely motivated young people working nonstop to invent a new, electronic universe amidst inexpensive yet stimulating interiors that appeared to be non-hier-archical, team-based, collaborative and—yes—fun. This kind of workplace can outperform its predecessors can be seen at the Digital Media Campus, in El Segundo, California, designed by Aref & Associates. In a converted warehouse space comprising a 50,000-square foot ground floor and 5,000-square foot mezzanine for over 300 employees in a commercial and industrial neighborhood anchored by Los Angeles International Airport, the Internet and new media business has developed a tightly-knit community

Above: *Main Street with Waterfall by Eric Orr.*
Left: *Commons on mezzanine.*
Upper left: *Internet kiosks and plasma screen TVs in reception.*

of private offices, teaming work stations, conference rooms, team rooms, Zen room, computer room and mezzanine-level commons area. Senior management is always accessible to the staff at the hub of the space via a "Main Street" corridor, and employees move freely through a highly functional setting whose innovative use of materials retains the capacity to inspire and delight—virtues in economies new or old.

A/R Environetics Group, Inc.

116 East 27 Street
New York
New York 10016
212.679.8100
212.685.9044 (Fax)
www.arenvironetics.com
info@arenvironetics.com

A/R Environetics Group, Inc.

Ask Jeeves, Inc.
New York, New York

They're an odd yet charming couple: Ask.com, a California-based Web site that directs visitors to other Web sites for assistance, and Jeeves, a service mark based on British author P.G. Wodehouse's unflappable butler for fumbling aristocrat Bertie Wooster. Though Web surfers seldom know who Jeeves is, they understand the site the moment the butler's image appears. The ability to put people at ease is also evident in Ask Jeeves's functional and charming, 13,200-square foot New York office for 60 employees, designed by A/R Environetics Group. The situation that preceded the facility is familiar to dot-coms everywhere: a small staff in a single room building, an Internet presence and hiring staff rapidly. An airy space was created in a loft with pinwheel-clustered open plan work stations surrounding the columns, elliptical equipment stands for overflow work space, and enclosed conference rooms. Strong colors derived from the company's website enhance the playful environment. Jeeves might even loosen his well-starched collar here.

Above: Work stations and equipment stands. *Right:* Work station cluster around column. *Far right:* "Ask Jeeves" logo at reception desk. *Opposite:* Reception and conference room. *Photography:* David Joseph.

A/R Environetics Group, Inc.

Comprehensive Quotes and Graphics (CQG)
New York, New York

Above: General office area.
Below: Reception.
Right: Employee lounge.
Photography: David Joseph.

The typical Wall Street trading room is a frantic, noisy and crowded world filled with high-strung, high-volume and high-paid people. However, it's a familiar place to traders, and the offices of Comprehensive Quotes and Graphics, designed by A/R Environetics Group and located in New York's financial district, capture the look if not necessarily the adrenaline rush that makes them feel at home. A similar affect can be discerned in the new 7,500-square foot office for 17 employees. CQG provides market data to high-octane traders whose access to timely financial statistics can spell the difference between profit and loss, so the company has recreated the traders' environment as its own workplace. Not only does the office provide functional space for employees, it presents the company's software in a familiar setting, right down to the open, ordered trading desks. A segmented curved wall of corrugated aluminum panels defines areas with wooden soffits and light boxes at entry points without using doors, further enhancing the open environment.

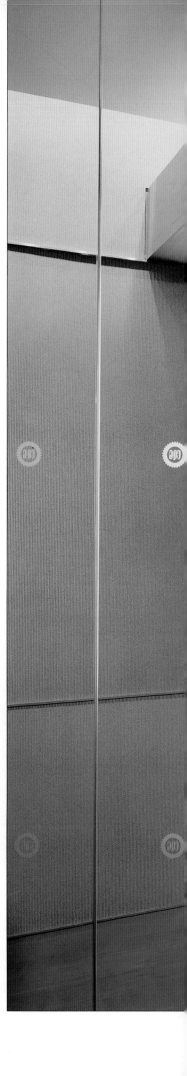

A/R Environetics Group, Inc.

Capital Management Firm
New York, New York

Change has come swiftly to the financial world as deregulation, globalization, and the development of powerful information technologies move capital around the globe at the speed of electrons and photons. As a result, the workplace inhabited by bankers, brokers and their colleagues has made room for an arsenal of computers, printers and other office machines. Yet the financial world proudly retains its memory of centuries-old traditions. A recently completed, 18,000-square foot office for a capital management firm in New York, designed by A/R Environetics Group, illustrates how gracefully past and present can converge. An interior sweeping curved wall encloses the reception area, trading room and technology center allowing the few offices, conference rooms and multitude of open plan low workstations full access to light and open views. Everything is defined by an architecture of exotic hardwoods, limestone, fine millwork and metalwork that is timeless.

A/R Environetics Group, Inc.

Private Fitness Facility
New York, New York

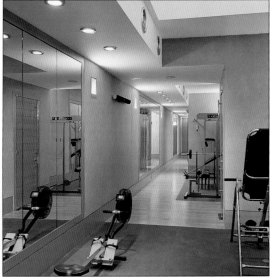

Executive suite. Executive dining. Executive washroom. Why don't Americans resent the perquisites of power? They want them too. Whatever else can be said for the 1,800-square foot private fitness facility designed for a Manhattan business by A/R Environetics Group, it packs a lot of activity into a tight urban space. Atop a low-rise commercial building, users of the facility can find a skylit free-weight area, aerobic room, yoga area, steam room, massage rooms, showers and juice bar. A/R Environetics Group created an environment of contrast-cool "concrete" panel walls vs. warm cedar wood floor, custom doors and millwork. If young people need good reasons to succeed in business, this space has to be one.

Above left: Showers with steam and dressing rooms.
Above right: View towards free-weight area.
Top right: Juice bar/Yoga area.
Below right: Aerobic room.
Photography: David Joseph.

Berger Rait

411 Fifth Avenue
New York
New York 10016
212.993.9000
212.993.9001 (Fax)
www.bergerrait.com

Berger Rait

Offices of Berger Rait
New York, New York

The employees of Berger Rait have reasons to be grateful for their recent move to a 10,000-square foot, one-floor studio in midtown Manhattan. Clients find the new location easy to reach, for example, and Grand Central Station and other sources of mass transit are right nearby. Better yet, the bright and airy facility that the designers have created represents a substantial increase in space and efficiency over the crowded, two-floor facility in the Wall Street area they left behind, and the interior design is regarded by clients as a showcase of ideas they can use for their own projects. The elegant, modernist environment evolved from the firm's needs and a desire to create a space that allows Berger Rait to explore its own issues

of working, productivity and communication. The design exploits existing conditions in the new location, including high ceilings, large structural columns and concrete floors. As a result, all eyes focus on the design studio as centerpiece, surrounded by partner and administrative offices with sliding glass and metal doors on one wall and elevators and support services on two others, exposing one long wall to daylight and views. Visitors respond to the design positively, coming away with creative ideas that may have direct application to their own facilities.

Left: *Conference room.*
Above: *Reception.*
Opposite above: *Design studio.*
Opposite below: *Administrative and Private office area.*
Photography: *Mark Ross.*

Berger Rait

Data Broadcasting Corporation
New York, New York

Below: Reception.
Photography: Peter Paige.

Right: Conference room.
Below right: Private office.

Data Broadcasting Corporation is a leading global provider of financial and business information to institutional and individual investors, supplying time-sensitive pricing, dividend, corporate action and descriptive information for over 3.5 million securities around the world, including hard-to-value unlisted fixed income instruments. One of its products, eSignal, is the leading real-time, Internet-delivered subscription quote service for traders, offering charts, news, research and alerts direct to a laptop, PC or telephone. Consequently, when the company retained Berger Rait to design its 30,000-square foot, full-floor facility in midtown Manhattan, it requested a modern and forward-looking environment that would project an impressive corporate presence. The resulting space, including reception, open plan work areas, conference rooms, media/presentation rooms for sales and technical training, and an executive suite, is highlighted by the reception area's display wall with TV screens and a ticker tape for visitor viewing. There's no reason to look less than a leader when you are one, as Data Broadcasting Corporation knows.

Berger Rait

barnesandnoble.com
New York, New York

Above: *Meeting rooms.*
Right: *Interior staff meeting room.*
Opposite: *Reception.*
Photography: *Peter Paige.*

What's it like growing from a small, start-up Internet operation with an aggressive business plan to an organization of 400 employees requiring 92,000 square feet of office and support facilities in two phases on a single floor? The new Manhattan home of barnesandnoble.com, the offspring of bookseller Barnes & Noble, has been designed by Berger Rait as a largely open-plan environment with private offices on the perimeter and meeting and break areas distributed off a main corridor. The facility embraces its industrial surroundings by leaving the 14-foot ceiling mostly open and dramatically illuminated by pendant lighting fixtures, contrasting unadorned concrete structure with color accents on feature walls, carpet tile and work station tack surfaces, and exposing ducts and utilities in suspended racks.

Right: Cafeteria.
Below left: Open plan area.

Equally important, however, are details that enliven open plan work stations, private offices, meeting rooms, break areas and cafeteria, including a glass and metal grid system for perimeter offices, translucent wall panels for interior staff meeting rooms, a suspended metal mesh curtain for the cafeteria, attractive contemporary furnishings, colorful textiles and carpeting, and a direct/indirect lighting design. While design can't eliminate growing pains, it certainly eases the way for barnesandnoble.com.

Bergmeyer Associates, Inc.

Bergmeyer Associates, Inc.
Architecture and Interiors
286 Congress Street
Boston
Massachusetts 02210
617.542.1025
617.338.6897 (Fax)
www.bergmeyer.com
info@bos.bergmeyer.com

Bergmeyer Associates, Inc.

CGN Marketing and Creative Services
Boston, Massachusetts

Natural light floods the 13,750-square foot office of CGN Marketing and Creative Services in Boston, Massachusetts—adding form, color and drama to a spare yet warm modern environment. Designed by Bergmeyer, the simplicity is in keeping with the client's program for this project, and marries well with the re-use of existing built elements. The designer introduced "light fins" at conference rooms to provide visual privacy from the lobby and allow natural light to bathe the corridor. Birch framed translucent screens and doors were introduced as a motif to give enclosure to workstations while extending vistas throughout the entire office for this 55-person marketing communications company. Indirect and recessed lighting fixtures, coupled with exterior light, illuminate walls in the private offices, open plan workstations and conference rooms. The reception/waiting area with its light maple woods and translucent screens includes an understated coffee bar where CGN serves such clients as Amtrak, Fidelity Investments, Massachusetts Office of Travel & Tourism and Salomon Smith Barney. The use of strong geometry, long and short views and a simple but warm color palette give the space its sophisticated but casually cool tone.

Above left: Circulation.
Above right: Meeting area.
Right: Light fins.
Opposite: Conference room.
Photography: Lucy Chen.

Bergmeyer Associates, Inc.

Intex Solutions, Inc.
Needham, Massachusetts

It's one thing to fall in love with a warehouse. It's another to transform one at a Needham, Massachusetts office park into a 23,000-square foot office for 70 employees of Intex Solutions, a provider of timely and comprehensive data, models and related software for the structured fixed-income market. Because Intex wanted to retain the warehouse space, Bergmeyer rotated the floor plan 45 degrees to the building grid. The private offices and custom work stations of departments, product assembly, computer and conference rooms are gathered around a central skylit "piazza", much like a medieval Italian city. Custom free-standing screens used instead of furniture system panels, a garage door that expands the main conference room, and the landscaped "piazza" for informal meetings and dining are special features that give Intex one truly exceptional warehouse.

Above: *Exterior.*
Left: *Reception.*
Lower left: *Piazza.*
Opposite: *Open plan work stations with screens.*
Photography: *Lucy Chen.*

Bergmeyer Associates, Inc.

NerveWire
Newton,
Massachusetts

Above: *Circulation and informal meeting spaces.*
Right: *Reception area.*
Below left: *Typical team room.*

How do you satisfy an organization whose need for shelter embraces lively public forums and quiet intimate places, openness and privacy, team effort and individual tasks, and new and old economy clients—while simultaneously reinforcing its brand and supporting its team-based delivery of services? This was the challenge posed by NerveWire in Newton, Massachusetts, the site of the company's new, 54,000-square foot, three-level office for 244 employees. NerveWire is a management consulting and systems integration firm that focuses on inter-enterprise integration to assist clients in envisioning and building business models that connect their strategies, people, processes and technologies internally as well as with those of their customers and suppliers. To fulfill its complex requirements for the workplace,

4

Right: Waiting area for reception.
Photography: Lucy Chen.

Bergmeyer carefully structured the high-tech environment to achieve a dynamic balance among contrasting conditions. As a result, private offices, open work spaces, project team rooms, formal and informal meeting areas, training room, computer rooms, kitchens and dining spaces, and game room give NerveWire employees countless spatial options whatever their assignments may be. Such telling details as glass conference room walls with frosted bands, project team rooms with sliding doors, meeting spaces of varying sizes and degrees of privacy, and furnishings that reflect both conventional and contemporary tastes help NerveWire bridge the shifting distances between its many worlds.

Above: Main kitchen and dining area.
Left: Typical conference room.
Right: Typical circulation path.

Bottom Duvivier

2603 Broadway
Redwood City
California 94063
650.361.1209
650.361.1229 (Fax)
www.b-d.com
info@b-d.com

Bottom Duvivier

Deloitte Consulting LLP
San Francisco, California

Above: *Quiet room.*
Right: *Cafe Lisa.*
Below: *Boardroom.*
Opposite:
Reception/gathering space.
Photography: *Cesar Rubio.*

Good management consultants are out of the office—serving clients. Since Deloitte Consulting LLP's consultants in San Francisco are out 80 percent of the time, Bottom Duvivier faced an intriguing problem in designing their new, 40,000-square foot facility. How do you design a superior environment for 340 employees split between consultants on the go and administrative and support staff remaining in the office? In an innovative twist, the reception/gathering space, boardroom, partners' offices, and administrative/support staff "super service center" offer more space, storage and amenity to administrative and support personnel. Consultants' offices no longer ring the perimeter, all offices are "hotelled" as needed, and the central gathering space incorporates all major support services. "The result is a Deloitte Consulting office that we are very proud of," comments Leah Swiler, Deloitte's director of facilities. It's also a facility that works well coming—or going.

Bottom Duvivier

RealNames Corporation
Redwood City, California

Internet-related ventures have made a lasting impression on the business world through their worker-friendly facilities, the hothouses for twentysomethings that dramatically show how work spaces can be attractive, comfortable and "fun" as well as functional and cost-effective. A fascinating example is the 53,000-square foot, two-story facility for RealNames Corporation in Redwood City, California, by

Bottom Duvivier with United Kingdom-based Blauel Architects to consciously recruit and retain talented personnel in a competitive job market. The facility is breezily open in its private offices, work stations, team collaboration spaces and meeting rooms, boardroom, "quiet rooms," secured server rooms, cafeteria and recreational facility. To accentuate this quality, the design exposes the ceiling and suspend-

ed mechanical and electrical equipment, makes the walls seem transparent with translucent, backlit polycarbonate panels, and appoints the interiors in simple, handsome and versatile furnishings. RealNames all but proclaims that bright, talented, hard-working people are welcome here.

Left: Cafeteria.
Above: Single-height open plan office area.
Above left: Boardroom.
Opposite: Double-height open plan office area.
Photography: Cesar Rubio.

Left: *Main employee entrance.*
Below left: *Main assembly and test space.*

Top: *Main dining space.*
Above: *Fitness center lobby.*
Opposite: *Main public entrance.*
Photography: *Cesar Rubio, Mert Carpenter.*

One of the most successful computer companies long before the Internet's arrival has been Sun Microsystems, whose CEO Scott McNealy predicted, "The network is the computer," years ago. Sustaining this feisty and innovative spirit is a common goal in Sun's facilities, including the handsome new, million-square foot, seven-building Newark Campus for 3600 employees in Newark, California, where Bottom Duvivier provided master planning and interior design services. It's not your everyday office park. A primary objective has been to locate engineering close to manufacturing, producing an open but secure workplace where manufacturing is an integral part of operations. Consequently, Bottom Duvivier has created a flexible campus facility that adapts easily to changing manufacturing processes and fosters an informal collegiality in keeping with Sun's egalitarian culture. In a recent survey, employees overwhelmingly expressed their satisfaction with the facility—exceeding even their optimistic employer's expectations.

Bottom Duvivier   Sun Microsystems Santa Clara Conference Center Santa Clara, California

Left: *Grand Auditorium.*
Above: *Conference/ training room.*
Top: *Auditorium exterior.*
Below: *Main entry hall, Director's Mansion.*
Photography: *Alan Rosenberg.*

Architects praise buildings that exhibit "good bones," sturdy and serviceable structures whose floor plans, sections and basic architectural elements are likely to endure as their occupants and uses change. A living testimony to this concept is the new Sun Microsystems Santa Clara Conference Center in Santa Clara, California, in which Bottom Duvivier was interior design consultant. Two buildings, a 6,973-square foot mansion built in 1888 and a newer, 16,585-square foot adjoining auditorium, were renovated to provide a corporate events facility for Sun Microsystems during business hours Monday through Friday, and a public venue for the City of Santa Clara on evenings and weekends. The ample structures accommodated a varied program that included an auditorium, conference and training rooms, breakout room, private offices, boardroom, servery kitchen and main entry hall. Functional and flexible as the new center is, it also displays a pride of place that only "good bones" can instill.

Brayton & Hughes Design Studio

639 Howard Street
San Francisco
California 94105
415.291.8100
415.434.8145 (Fax)
www@bhdstudio.com
info@bhdstudio.com

Brayton & Hughes
Design Studio

A Global Consulting Firm
Los Angeles, California

Above: Conference room.
Right: Entry lobby.
Opposite: Lobby desk and firm timeline.
Below: Private office.
Photography: Toshi Yoshimi.

How often do consultants consult each other? At the Los Angeles office of a 70-year-old global consulting firm whose alumni head many of the world's greatest companies, investigation revealed that its key personnel had minimal interaction. The nature of the business didn't help, since consulting keeps high-powered employees out of the office. Yet the office itself was not particularly supportive. People generally remained within mentorship groups rather than client teams, or worked individually when they came to the office. To stimulate more interaction as well as promote better work among 165 employees, the firm retained Brayton & Hughes to design the renovation and expansion of 45,000 square foot of existing space on several floors. Brayton & Hughes placed "pods" containing living rooms, kitchens and conference spaces amidst general office areas of individual work modules, decentralized support activities such as fax, copier and supply storage, and modified interconnecting stairs to encourage daily use. The consulting firm notes that the new environment is so enticing, job candidates want to jump right in.

Brayton & Hughes
Design Studio

A Global Consulting Firm
Palo Alto, California

One of the world's top consulting firms had two potentially incompatible goals for its new, 40,000-square foot office, designed by Brayton & Hughes in Palo Alto, California. Such are the economics of consulting that the firm wanted an appealing environment of natural light and scenic views for 195 employees—along with efficient, high density floors to accommodate the firm's annual recruitment objectives in Silicon Valley. The architect's solution included the organization of dense work station clusters along gracious circulation paths, the use of opposing visual elements, such as laminated glass, wood and perforated metal, to symbolize Silicon Valley's transition from pastoral orchards to high-technology leadership, and the introduction of attractive internal destinations, including an employee cafe, among the private offices, team rooms, video conference rooms and large hall. Not only does the design meet its objectives, it has produced images that are not easily forgotten, including a lobby stairwell defined by a monumental sculpture of eight trees depicting Silicon Valley's unspoiled past. That turns heads even in the virtual world.

Brayton & Hughes
Design Studio

Silver Lake Partners
Menlo Park, California

Above: *Private office.*
Right: *Reception area.*
Photography: *John Sutton.*

Best in class does not have to shout. Accordingly, Silver Lake Partners has no wish to overstate its prominence as the leading private equity fund manager focused on technology. Accordingly, the firm retained Brayton & Hughes to design an 11,261-square foot office for 24 employees in Menlo Park, California, as an environment of "understated confidence" where visitors could be received, work requiring privacy and concentration could be performed, and informal meetings among colleagues could be held.

The key spatial concept that makes the space succeed is the crescent-shaped reception area from which all conference facilities branch off. Grouping these accommodations in a compact cluster lets the firm separate public and private activities, giving the partners flexibility to participate in meetings—or retreat discreetly to their private offices, aided by administrative staff in open plan areas and support services in the building core.

Below left: *Conference room.*
Opposite: *Elevator lobby and reception desk.*

Brayton & Hughes
Design Studio

Cooley Godward LLP
Palo Alto, California

With construction and furnishing to be completed in just 120 days on a stringent budget, the design of the 130,000-square foot, two-story office by Brayton & Hughes for 450 employees of the Palo Alto, California-based law firm Cooley Godward focused on key spaces. Obviously, the facility had to be functional and flexible, so a floor plan of eight distinct but interconnected suites was devised to let the firm easily sublet unneeded space. However, it would also be supportive, providing a maximum number of window offices for attorneys and a cafe to link everyone together, since

Cooley Godward's focus on business and litigation services for the technology sector has made it one of California's largest law firms. Emphasizing the appeal of the main entry lobby, typical open office area and the cafe has paid off by establishing a high visual standard for the entire facility that speaks of quality rather than expediency.

Above left: Reception.
Above right: Cafe seating.
Right: Open office area.
Below right: Cafe servery.
Photography: John Sutton.

Carrier Johnson

1301 Third Avenue
San Diego
California 92101
619.239.2353
619.239.6227 (Fax)
www.carrierjohnson.com

2600 Michelson Drive
Suite 400
Irvine
California 92612
949.955.2353
949.955.2377 (Fax)

855 Sansome Street
Suite 302
San Francisco
California 94111
415.772.8200
415.772.8201 (Fax)

Carrier Johnson

NeoPoint
San Diego, California

Left: General office area.
Below left: Executive conference room.
Below: Lunch/game room.
Opposite: Think Tank.
Photography: Anne Garrison, David Hewitt.

Wireless offices have proved as unlikely as paperless offices at the dawn of the 21st century, but the sight of young and old communicating via an array of wireless devices around the globe confirms that a new market is thriving. The potential of the technology helps explain the excitement at the new, 103,000-square foot, two-building campus in San Diego designed by Carrier Johnson for NeoPoint, a wireless communications company. To stimulate the exchange of information, NeoPoint makes casual encounters easy and appealing for its employees. Each two-story structure focuses on its "Think Tank," a first-floor activity center open to the second floor from which open plan work stations, perimeter private offices, conference rooms, laboratories, training room, lunchroom and fitness center radiate. Each "Tank" comes with comfortable furniture, central staircase, coffee bar and other enticements for young, high-energy techies who crave coffee and enjoy brainstorming sessions around the clock. When major advances come to wireless communications, places like NeoPoint will power them.

Carrier Johnson

Peregrine Systems
San Diego, California

Since many information technology (IT) goods and services did not exist even six months ago, it's not surprising that Peregrine Systems, a specialist in infrastructure management software, recently built an 8,205-square foot Executive Briefing Center (EBC), designed by Carrier Johnson, as the centerpiece of its 440,000-square foot San Diego headquarters. Explaining how the fitness of an organization's IT infrastructure, operating via computers, networks, telephone systems, buildings and transportation fleets, can ultimately determine success or failure takes considerable effort when the audience consists of Fortune 500 executives who are not necessarily chief information officers (CIOs). Peregrine conducts a major initiative to educate potential customers at the EBC. Using a choreographed sequence of spaces and displays starting at the entry, with its view of the Demo Lab, proceed-

ing through a series of interactive exhibits and breakout areas where potential customers and marketing representatives meet, and concluding at the 30-seat Executive Theater, where state-of-the-art presentations are given. Lunch is served in the executive dining room against a digital display wall depicting Peregrine's e-commerce projects. Customer Focus Rooms are where executives learn how Peregrine can tailor its software to their specific needs. For Peregrine, one EBC is worth thousands of words.

Right: *Entry to Executive Briefing Center.*
Above: *Interactive display.*
Photography: *Anne Garrison, David Hewitt.*

Right: Executive Theater.
Below right: Open office area.

Carrier Johnson

Hilton Gaslamp Quarter
San Diego, California

Below: Main lobby and entry.
Bottom: Check-in desk.
Photography: Anne Garrison, David Hewitt.

Founded in 1769, the heart of downtown San Diego's gaslamp district is now a vibrant tourist and resident destination. With a perfect year-round climate this district is a haven for tourism and a bonus for downtown professionals. For this reason, S.D. Malkin Properties takes pride in this development as it generously respects its historic context while providing a significant architectural addition for the San Diego resident. This 253-room Hilton Gaslamp departs from its predictable generic hotel design and instead, synthesizes 19th century industrial elements from the shipping industry with the elegance of contemporary Southern California design. Symbolic reminders of the warehouse and wharf structures are transformed into restaurants, bars, retail and conference rooms of the hotel. In addition, an outdoor elevated 'ArtWalk' provides an active social space while gathering the various components and layers of the entire project. The result is a boutique hotel and a retail/mixed-use block that collaborate to form a wealth of amenities for the business traveler as well as the San Diego resident.

Above: Dining room and bar.
Opposite: Fireplace lounge.

Carrier Johnson

Motorola
San Diego, California

To provide security for isolated research and development laboratories while also creating a highly interactive office environment in one building was the design challenge for Carrier Johnson. The 327,000 sf corporate campus for the Broadband Communications Sector of Motorola, Inc. sited on the rim of a spectacular canyon in San Diego, complete with cafeteria and health club, meets this challenge head on. Laboratories strategically occupy interior core space, while offices, conference rooms and employee amenities are placed appropriately on the perimeter. Expansive corridors, lobbies and outdoor landscaped paths thread their way through the interiors and grounds so adeptly that employees are supported by environments that enhance all aspects of company operations. Who would believe that secured laboratory buildings could be infused by natural light and views of a canyon landscape? Motorola employees, for sure.

Davis · Carter · Scott

805 15th Street NW
Suite 1100
Washington DC 20005
202.682.2300
202.789.2852 (Fax)
www.dcsdesign.com

1676 International Drive
Suite 500
McLean
Virginia 22102
703.556.9275
703.821.6976 (Fax)

Davis ▪ Carter ▪ Scott

Xpedior
Alexandria, Virginia

Below: Elevator lobby with view of lounge/lunchroom. **Photography:** Gunnar Westerlind.

Even Internet ventures eventually raise their sights beyond impromptu workplaces, as Xpedior has in developing a 50,000 square foot office in Alexandria, Virginia, designed by Davis Carter Scott. The innovative Internet and e-business firm wanted the 235-person facility to express its "bold, imaginative, adventurous and professional" persona. The design offers floor plans with walls set at varying angles to the building grid, open plan areas deploying team-oriented, seven-station pods, conference rooms at the corners, and a state-of-the-art training center. The space also features amenities such as a game room with casual seating, large-screen TV and pool table, a café-style lounge/lunchroom, a "Think Tank" and other unusual meeting places, and "touchdown" spaces for visiting clients, guests and staff from other offices. Chol Kong, Manager of Operations for Xpedior, observes, "Our office conveys what we want people to know about our company.... We have a lot of fun doing what we do."

Above: Reception area.
Right: Lounge/lunch-room with view of game room.

91

Davis • Carter • Scott

Mark G. Anderson Consultants
Washington, D.C.

A six-week whirlwind of design and construction from "kick-off" meeting to move-in, a shoestring budget, and the desire for innovative, funky design were all the right reasons for Washington D.C. based Mark G. Anderson Consultants to hire Davis Carter Scott to design their corporate offices. The space includes private offices, open work places, a copy/pantry room and conference rooms ... and utilizes fundamental design elements such as lighting, color, and distinctive furnishings — including a motorized, metal garage door — to stretch the budget and bring the office to life. Because the space wraps around a central atrium, its floor plan fully exploits the natural light by positioning private offices on the interior, and public corridors and administrative staff workstations on the perimeter. The impact of bold, primary colors and stylish, contemporary furnishings is considerable. Rebecca Wilson, Principal, reports that, "the first word of everyone's month is 'Wow!'"

Right: Conference room with view to atrium.
Opposite: Open work places.
Photography: Gunnar Westerlind.

Davis ▪ Carter ▪ Scott

Inktomi Corporation
Herndon, Virginia

Below: Briefing center corridor with demonstration room and visitors' cafe.
Photography: Gunnar Westerlind.

Developing a facility with numerous programmatic requirements to satisfy a leader in Internet infrastructure would be formidable under normal circumstances. However, San Francisco-based Inktomi Corporation was in a rush to open its 25,000 square foot office for 85 employees in Herndon, Virginia just outside of Washington, D.C. Davis Carter Scott's design staff worked closely with Inktomi, beginning with a "Town Hall Meeting" to jump-start the programming phase. What typically involves one-on-one meetings and takes three weeks to complete, was accomplished as a group in three hours.

Above: *Cylindrical "think tank" serving open plan area.*
Top: *Private office.*

95

The space features a high-tech reception area, a conference/briefing center, demonstration rooms, a visitors' café, private offices, open plan workstations, a computer lab, library, game room and pantry. The finished interiors visually interpret Inktomi's mission — to develop and market scalable Internet applications so users can readily obtain information from the Web — through geometry, scale and color to create spaces as palpable objects. A measure of this facility's success was Davis Carter Scott being named to design Inktomi's 400,000 square foot headquarters in San Francisco. Reports Tom Masles, Inktomi's Director of Operations, "We're having just as much fun on this project!"

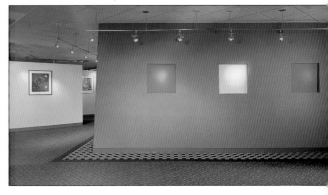

Top: *Reception area.*
Above right: *Game room exterior..*
Above: *"Touchdown station" for visitors and employees on the road.*

DMJM Rottet

3250 Wilshire Boulevard
Los Angeles
California 90010.1599
213.368.2888
213.381.2773 (Fax)
dmjmrottet@dmjm.com

DMJM Rottet

Deloitte & Touche
Los Angeles, California

Below: Board room.
Opposite top: Reception.
Opposite center:
Breakout area.
Opposite bottom:
Conference room.
Photography: Nick
Merrick @ Hedrich Blessing.

Can a dynamic organization develop a superior environment for growth and change? That's what the Los Angeles office of accounting firm Deloitte & Touche and its architect DMJM Rottet accomplished in developing a 350,000 square foot headquarters on 14 floors in one of the city's finest downtown highrises. The new facility simultaneously consolidates Deloitte's offices, reduces real estate costs, and creates a more appropriate and efficient workplace for employees. Based on Deloitte's one standard private office and one standard open plan work station, the design introduces an easily modified floor plan template featuring perimeter offices whose translucent glass walls flood the interiors with daylight, a state-of-the-art conference floor with multi-purpose facilities, numerous other flexible spaces and an aggressive hoteling program. Here growth and change are welcome—by design.

**Unocal Corporation
El Segundo, California**

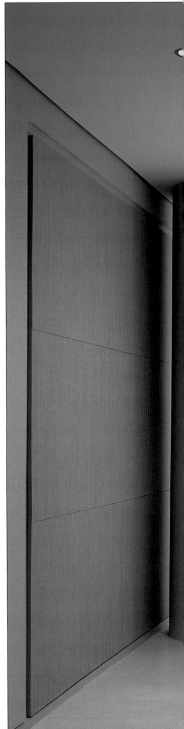

Above: *Prefunction area.*
Left: *Main boardroom.*
Right: *Reception*
Photography: *Nick Merrick @ Hedrich Blessing.*

To accommodate its growing international trade, the multinational oil company Unocal relocated its executive headquarters from downtown Los Angeles to new 80,000 square foot offices in El Segundo, close to Los Angeles International Airport. The facility, designed by DMJM Rottet, accommodates executives and related support groups as well as an increasing number of visiting and traveling employees in a space wrapped around an inner courtyard. This arrangement, configured as a doughnut-shaped plan, achieves a flexible layout at minimal cost. Along with operational flexibility and stringent cost controls, Unocal's other priority requirements included disaster recovery war rooms and extensive, state-of-the-art teleconferencing and video-conferencing facilities. The main boardroom and teleconferencing room are adjacent to a large prefunction area, kitchen facilities and office service center as well as the reception area, so Unocal can host client functions and presentations without disturbing private office areas, while offices for visiting executives are strategically located in triangular rooms where corridors meet. Unocal's new home office is mission-ready long before anyone boards a plane or disembarks from one.

DMJM Rottet

Steelcase Wood Furniture Showroom
Chicago, Illinois

Intent on dispelling the myth that wood furniture is "too stuffy" for today's fast-paced work environment, Steelcase Wood Furniture selected DMJM Rottet to create an impressive 6,000 square foot showroom in Chicago's Merchandise Mart to inspire visitors to re-think the traditional notion of wood furniture. The design team relied on numerous environmental-themed design elements as well as the beauty of the furniture manufacturer's diverse product collections to create a persuasive setting that unfolds like a visual narrative from the moment a visitor enters. The entrance wall, for example, is lined with a light slot in the ceiling plane mirrored by a ground floor opening of natural stones. Floating "clouds" of gypsum ceiling and translucent wall paneling create unique planes and lighting schemes with custom-designed metal frame lighting suspended in the central space, while a three-screen video projection system expresses Steelcase Wood's commitment to fulfilling client needs and anchors the showroom. Does anyone think wood furniture is "too stuffy" now?

Above: The Tableau Collection of casegoods, designed by Lauren Rottet, Richard Riveire, and Kai Broms of DMJM.
Right: View of show-room over plinth.
Opposite center: Conference room.
Opposite left: Detail of showroom entry.
Photography: George Lambros Photography Inc.

DMJM Rottet

First Chicago West Coast Regional Office
Los Angeles, California

Right: Reception.
Below: Conference room.
Photography: Joe Aker, Aker/Zvonkoric Photography LLP.

First National Bank of Chicago or "First Chicago," America's oldest nationally chartered bank, serves clients in nine states west of the Rockies from its West Coast regional office in Los Angeles. In a move to a 20,000 square foot space in 777 South Figueroa, a prestigious building designed by Cesar Pelli with an efficient, nearly rectangular floorplate, the Bank asked DMJM Rottet to create an open atmosphere for its mostly private offices. The solution combines standard aluminum storefront components with etched glass as an interior curtainwall. Though there are no fancy finishes and little millwork because of the modest budget, the quality of the space comes through in the simplicity of the design, the abundant natural light, and the benefits of the generous floorplate.

Ellerbe Becket

800 LaSalle Avenue
Minneapolis
Minnesota 55402
612.376.2000
612.376.2271 (Fax)
www.ellerbebecket.com
info@ellerbebecket.com

Ellerbe Becket

Amtrak CNOC
Wilmington, Delaware

No, this isn't a dot-com story. When Amtrak's new Consolidated National Operations Center, designed by Ellerbe Becket, moved into a 52,000-square foot former warehouse in Wilmington, Delaware, it united six strategic business units in an open plan environment with universal work stations, glass-fronted private offices off the perimeter, team spaces in the center, and such amenities as the Conference Center, breakrooms, fitness center and outdoor dining terrace. The design features curving walls, bright colors and modern furnishings. Amtrak loves the results: employee retention is higher than expected, satisfaction with the 24/7 facility is overwhelming, employee absenteeism is down and communication between work groups is improving dramatically. As Amtrak shifts from a departmental structure to a cross-functional one, the CNOC will easily keep it on track.

Ellerbe Becket

Crescendo Ventures
Palo Alto, California

Who in Silicon Valley wouldn't thrill to be immersed in a cool industrial-style work environment? Not everyone, it seems. When Crescendo Ventures, a global venture capitalist organization, asked Ellerbe Becket to design a 4,620-square foot office for 14 employees in Palo Alto, California to reflect its new surroundings in an historic building, it deliberately went against the trend. Most technology-related businesses in the region either look like hungry start-ups or approximate what could someday be labeled high-tech warehouse chic. After Crescendo Ventures' building was gutted back to the original architecture, most new areas requiring lower ceilings were grouped around the elevator core, letting space along the periphery take advantage of the height and windows. The new interiors, including private offices, conference rooms, reception area and restrooms, do more than honor their context. They actually help Crescendo Ventures stand out from competitors. Historic vernacular? Far out.

Left: Reception.
Above: Conference room.
Top: Partner's office.
Photography: Russell Abraham.

Ellerbe Becket

Hi-wire
Minneapolis, Minnesota

Customers aware of Hi-wire's passion for "unrelenting customer service" are delighted to visit the award-winning, 12,000-square foot facility for the full-service post-production house in Minneapolis, designed by Ellerbe Becket. Its success comes from the creative fulfillment of customers' needs. Though the eight editing suites occupy windowless interior space free from distractions, customers inside them have access to the staff of 12 via the adjoining main corridor, which functions as a main street, and they can also turn to a concierge station, laptop areas, fitness room and cafe with full-time chef for additional services and amenities. In addition, editing suites are vertically separated into two distinct zones, one where customers can work or relax, and another where technicians perform their services. Despite the long hours customers must often spend at Hi-wire, the environment assures them that "unrelenting customer service" can be a pleasurable experience.

Above left: *Cafe.*
Above right: *Reception.*
Top left: *Editing suite.*
Right: *Screening room.*
Photography: *Brian Droege.*

Ellerbe Becket

Metris Companies
Minnetonka, Minnesota

Below: *Executive reception area.*
Photography: *Dana Wheelock.*

Above left: General office floor.
Above right: Boardroom
Right: Private dining.

When you're hot, you're hot. Companies that grow rapidly because of customers' acceptance of their products or the desire to dominate the marketplace find that sudden success exacts a price. Consider the experience of Metris Companies, a relatively young organization offering credit card services. Its rapid growth—100 percent in each of the past few years—made the design of its 305,000-square foot, nine-floor expansion space in Minnetonka, Minnesota a special challenge to the archi-tecture firm of Ellerbe Becket. How do you make a work environ-ment comfortable and appealing yet functional and flexible to attract, house and retain a maxi-mum capacity of 1,100 employees, providing such standard facilities as an executive suite, open plan offices and conference center, as well as such extraordi-nary amenities as a full-service cafeteria, employee fitness center, on-site daycare center and on-site convenience store? The solution emphasizes appropriate-ness in each area.

The executive suite, for instance, is formal and impressive. By contrast, open plan office areas employ furniture systems chosen for utility and flexibility and disperse a variety of meeting spaces and alternative work settings. The cafeteria is light in scale and spirit to provide visual relief from everything else, and the daycare center is playful, colorful and scaled for children. Metris's CEO, Ronald N. Zebeck, has gratefully noted, "This facility is a reflection of Metris's past and future growth, and demonstrates the commitment we have made to our customers, employees and shareholders." At least one hot company is cool enough to take care of its employees as well as its customers.

Above: *Cafeteria.*
Right: *Daycare center.*

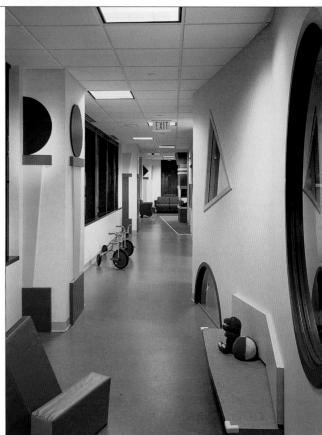

Francis Cauffman Foley Hoffmann, Architects Ltd.

2120 Arch Street
Philadelphia
Pennsylvania 19103
215.568.8250
215.568.2639 (Fax)
www.fcfh-did.com

Francis Cauffman Foley Hoffmann, Architects Ltd.

Fox, Rothschild, O'Brien & Frankel, LLP
Philadelphia, Pennsylvania

One of the cornerstones of Philadelphia history is its legal fraternity. Indeed, the archetype Philadelphia attorney has been a key figure in the city for generations. Yet even the law is subject to change, which can be readily appreciated in the 120,000-square foot law office for 300 employees of Fox, Rothschild, O'Brien & Frankel, renovated by Francis Cauffman Foley Hoffmann, Architects. The project involved creating a new overall image, central confer- ence center, intercon- necting staircase and upgraded lighting. Central conference cen- ters have become critical assets for law firms, giv- ing them and their clients superb facilities for critical meetings backed by state-of-the- art information technol- ogy. The fine example shown here, along with remodeled private offices, library, training, mail copy center, record storage and lunchroom, displays the new vigor of an august profession.

Above: *Reception seen from desk.*
Below: *Elevator lobby.*
Photography: *Don Pearse.*

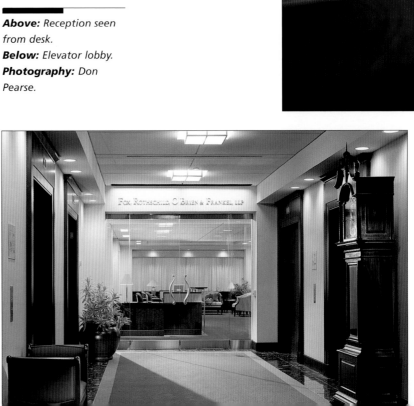

114

Above: *Reception for central conference center.*
Right: *Typical conference room.*

Francis Cauffman Foley Hoffmann, Architects Ltd.

Merck & Co., Inc.
Lansdale, Pennsylvania

Who could foresee the warehouse's multiple identity in today's economy? Yet the choice appears perfect for the 110,000-square foot U.S. Human Health Division Training & Professional Development Center of Merck & Co., Inc. in Lansdale, Pennsylvania, designed by Francis Cauffman Foley Hoffmann, Architects Ltd. for a projected staff of 150. Its 40-foot x 60-foot column bays and 15-foot ceilings lend themselves to 1500-square foot training rooms, breakout rooms, screening rooms, study area, cafeteria, and other facilities built or planned. The structure benefits from new mechanical and electrical systems, advanced audio/visual and information technology equipment, a new curtain wall system and courtyards that act as "town squares." The result is a superb training venue—former warehouse or not.

116

Francis Cauffman Foley Hoffmann, Architects Ltd.

AlliedSignal/Honeywell
Morristown, New Jersey

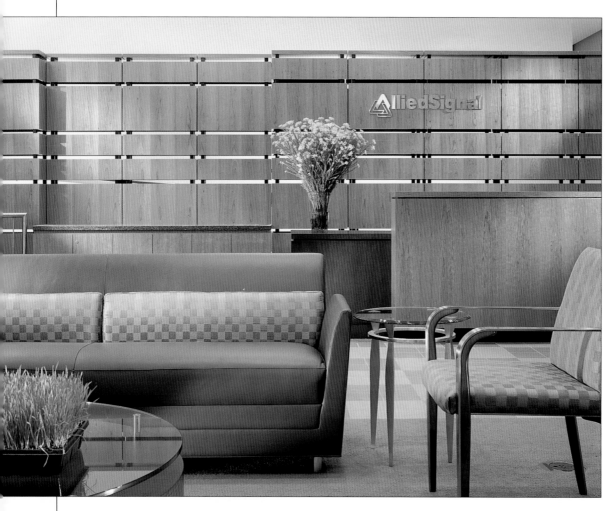

Good first impressions are what lobbies, foyers and reception areas are all about. Like the living room of a family residence, the lobby of a commercial or institutional building may be seen more in passing than in repose. However, the 4500-square foot central lobby for the Morristown, New Jersey campus of Allied Signal/Honeywell, a Fortune 500 company recently acquired by General Electric, illustrates how eloquent a first impression can be with a renovation designed by Francis Cauffman Foley Hoffmann, Architects. The building program reflects numerous concerns: a new ramp meeting ADA requirements, a new reception desk and visitors' seating, and upgrades to lighting, elevator cabs, security entrances and exterior site work. What matters to visitors, however, is that the handsome new central lobby, planned for high visibility with cherrywood, ceramic pavers, fine furniture and sophisticated light fixtures, greets them just as a dynamic and successful corporation of the 21st century should.

Francis Caufman Foley Hoffmann

University of Pennsylvania
Biomedical Research Building II/III
Philadelphia, Pennsylvania

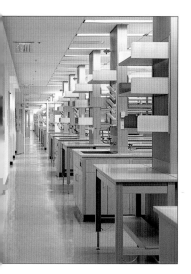

A serious game of musical chairs plays out in laboratory buildings worldwide as experiments start, finish or continue their pursuit of discovery. The process makes for rewarding science—and a major challenge to architecture that is deftly resolved in the University of Pennsylvania's 384,000-square foot Biomedical Research Building II/III, Philadelphia, Pennsylvania for 660 people. Whereas administrative offices can change with minimal disruption, laboratory modules require water, ventilation, gas and other critical service connections that are best left in place. To minimal disruption of occupied laboratory modules in the normal course of occupancy at Biomedical Research Building II/III, Francis Cauffman Foley Hoffmann, Architects introduced a generic plan for sequential fit out, flexible alcoves that enable principal investigator space to change size easily, and linear equipment corridors to sustain the flow of materials in and out. A laboratory is never "finished," but the University of Pennsylvania's example makes a virtue of impermanence.

Above: Conference room.
Left: Private office.
Upper left: Laboratory module.
Photography: Don Pearse.

Francis Cauffman Foley Hoffmann, Architects Ltd.

The Oaks Personal Care Facility Wyncote, Pennsylvania

The site was an abandoned stone gothic mansion from the late 1 gth century in a residential setting. The mansion had originally been built as a summer home for the Stetson Family of The Stetson Hat Company. Later in its history, the mansion had been converted into a nursing home with a one-story addition. This facility eventually closed due to code deficiencies in the increasingly regulated long-term care industry. The Genesis Eldercare's goal was to create a personal care facility for residents diagnosed with the early stages of Alzheimer's disease. They purchased the abandoned building determined that they wanted to create an affluent, traditional aesthetic with a hospitality influence, reflective of the neighborhood it resides in. The mansion itself provided great inspiration, serving as the hub of social activity spaces. Most of the ornate moldings and details original to the mansion were maintained with restoration, providing a strong sense of opulence to a project with a tight budget. Two, 2-story wings were added to the mansion, providing 49 Resident Rooms. The overall design theme was that of a

French Country Chateau. The challenge came in developing this kind of environment, keeping the special needs of dementia patients in mind all within what is otherwise considered a healthcare, institutional setting. The design team worked closely with the dementia specialists from Genesis to understand the visual and mental challenges common to elderly Alzheimer's patients. The range of items that required special consideration was vast.

Above: Great Hall and private dining room.
Right: Typical resident room.
Photography: Don Pearse.

120

Gary Lee Partners

360 West Superior Street
Chicago
Illinois 60610
312.640.8300
312.640.8301 (Fax)
www.garyleepartners.com

Gary Lee Partners

Russell Reynolds Associates
Chicago, Illinois

Above: Elevator lobby.
Above right: Private office.
Top right: Boardroom.
Opposite: Reception.
Photography:
Christopher Barrett/
Hedrich Blessing.

Expressing time-honored practices and unprecedented service commitment through architecture for this international executive recruiting firm's new offices was of primary importance. Accomplishing this while still providing for state of the art technologies was the challenge. The resulting design, developed by Gary Lee Partners, creates a sophisticated space through the blending of traditional architectural details with simple, modern lines. A sense of warmth and history are conveyed through the materials selected such as the use of velvet, leather, Satinwood and Corelean Burl veneers, and acid-etched glass. An eclectic collection of furniture and art work composed of textiles, paintings, photography, and paper pieces further compliments the architecture and contributes to the depth of the space. The new facilities accommodate more than 70 employees within 22,000 sf. Provisions include ample filing and production areas, food service zone, reception area, private offices adjacent to custom-designed support workstations and a Boardroom outfitted with a movable partition for flexibility. Private offices are configured as one standard size to eliminate the reconfiguration costs associated with personnel changes. The resulting space successfully communicates the firm's culture of traditional values with progressive business approaches through a functional, efficient and effective environment.

Gary Lee Partners

A Professional Services Firm
Chicago, Illinois

Lower left: *Club.*
Right: *Comfortable team room.*
Bottom left: *Cafe.*
Bottom right: *Exercise room.*
Photography: *Steve Hall/Hedrich Blessing.*

Gary Lee Partners provided master planning and design services to this professional services firm as contiguous expansion space became available. These new floors provided an opportunity to explore alternative workspaces and other specialty areas to promote team interaction and reflect the new work patterns its employees require. The design concept of the firm's existing space is based upon the International Style. Building upon this concept, Gary Lee Partners developed a sophisticated solution that incorporates light, texture, and form. Polished materials in flooring surfaces and crisp glass walls reflect light and expand the visible dimension of the space. Classic, sleek, modern furnishings covered in plush materials add tactile balance to the space as well as function as objects of art. Among the new amenities is a large, comfortable team room that hosts informal meetings; a "Club" area to accommodate large working groups with full "plug-in" access to the firm's network; a café-break out space; and a fitness center with weight room, aerobics room, and shower/locker facilities. The environment, both refined and functional, reflects this firm's efforts to provide the best workplace accommodations and improve their employees' quality of life.

Gary Lee Partners

Baker & Daniels
Indianapolis, Indiana

Left: Private office.
Below left: Elevator lobby.
Below right: Corridor.
Opposite: Boardroom.
Photography: Steve Hall/Hedrich Blessing

Baker & Daniels chose to manage growth by opening a new 36,000 square foot office located adjacent to the northern Indianapolis technology corridor. Accessibility played a major factor in selecting the site in this newly constructed office park. Proximity to a major Indianapolis expressway and to its technology-based clientele affords the firm an opportunity to create a more central location for meetings. This locale better serves the downtown Indianapolis headquarters, the firm's other offices throughout Indiana, and its ever-expanding client services. The new office is home to the firm's growing technology, real estate, and estate planning practice groups. This new office breaks from the dark-wood, traditional image established at the downtown headquarter office. A fresh, more modern tone establishes its image by utilizing a light color palette, glass, marble, and stainless steel materials. The qualities expressed by subtle graining in Tay veneer and the smooth, reflective glass further compliment the clean architecture and crisp detailing throughout. The firm's commitment to quality is evident in the modern, classic furnishings and custom furniture provided for this expansion.

Amenities for the new location included a two-story reception and Boardroom space accented with a marble feature wall. The perimeter wall accommodates private attorney offices outfitted with state of the art access to technology. Support workstations are custom designed with ample horizontal work-surface area to support a variety of functional and equipment needs. Filing is easily accessible and plentiful. The resulting environment serves to illustrate Baker & Daniels' willingness to respond to the needs of its clients while preserving their original ideals and values.

Above: Reception area.

Gensler

600 California Street
San Francisco
California 94108
415.433.3700
415.627.3737 (Fax)
www.gensler.com

Amsterdam
Arlington
Atlanta
Baltimore
Boston
Charlotte
Chicago
Dallas
Denver
Detroit
Hong Kong
Houston

LaCrosse
London
Los Angeles
New York
Newport Beach
Parsippany
San Francisco
San Jose
San Ramon
Seattle
Tokyo
Washington, DC

Gensler

Shaklee Corporation
Pleasanton, California

A manufacturer of nutritional, personal care, household, and home water treatment products sold to consumers through a worldwide network of independent distributors, Shaklee Corporation has come a long way since its founding by Dr. Forrest C. Shaklee in 1956. Yet Dr. Shaklee's belief in the power of nature and the power within one's self remains the foundation of the business that is now part of Yamanouchi Consumer Inc. His philosophy is also evident in the award-winning, 127,000-square foot Shaklee headquarters located in Pleasanton, CA, designed by Gensler. The lobby, open plan offices, conference center, theater/auditorium and public spaces are designed to express the company's credo of "harmony with nature." Offices, for example, are organized around two atriums that face north and act as light monitors, furnishings incorporate certified veneers and custom fabrics with images of plants used in Shaklee products, and fresh air issues from an integrated underfloor system in an environment that would surely please Dr. Shaklee.

Gensler

Eisner Communications
Baltimore, Maryland

Eisner Communications, one of the nation's leading independent advertising and communications agencies, wanted a space that would reflect their brand as idea creators and strategic brand builders. They knew they needed a dynamic environment to attract great thinkers and give them room to grow. Yet, as an active player in the Baltimore community for nearly 70 years, a standard office building couldn't have reflected Eisner's personality. When an opportunity came along to renovate an abandoned 1902 furniture factory to Class "A" status and National Historic Register guidelines, Eisner seized it. Eisner's new 50,000 sq. ft. space in the renovated Bagby Building is a strong contrast to their old department-focused workplace. Now, creative and account staff are grouped together in "brand factories" where they achieve dynamic collaboration and idea cross-pollination like never before. Authenticity and light permeate the space, as the building's old timber construction converges with recovered wood flooring, skylights, architectural metals, translucent fiberglass paneling on 2x4s, glass block and exposed brick. Steel catwalks connected to a monumental stair in the reception bring in more texture and transparency. It's a modern, high energy factory that's producing the excitement of new ideas.

Above left: Brand team area.
Above right: Building lobby.
Right: Converted elevator shaft.
Opposite: Reception stair.
Photography: Paul Warchol.

Gensler

Nikken, Inc.
Irvine, California

In 1973, Isamu Masuda envisioned a company to help people everywhere achieve total wellness. Two years later, his vision led to the formation of Nikken in Fukuoka, Japan. Nikken, the company, the wellness and magnetic therapy products, and the business strategy, was built upon Masuda's concept of "total wellness," encompassing five key areas of life, defined by Nikken as The Five Pillars of Health™: Healthy Body, Healthy Mind, Healthy Family, Healthy Society and Healthy Finances. Today, Nikken is one of the world's largest, fastest growing network marketing companies, with a state-of-the-art, 225,000-square foot world headquarters in Irvine, California, designed by Gensler to give visible form to its beliefs. What sets this striking facility apart is its visual expression of the organization's philosophy (its brand).

The headquarters is a cluster of five structures that combine harmoniously and work together in balance, using their qualitative and quantitative programs to delineate their shapes, volumes and finishes. Although the facility serves such diverse needs as the executive offices, call center, marketing/customer service, retail store, training center/auditorium and automated warehouse distribution center, it is unified by the central atrium, which nurtures communication and interaction. The integration of the interior design with the architecture and landscape reinforces its inside-out design, bringing a flood of daylight and views indoors—an inviting vision of total wellness fit for Nikken.

Top: Executive office.
Above: General office space.
Below: Training room.

Griswold, Heckel & Kelly Assoc., Inc. and Space/Management Programs

GHK
55 West Wacker Drive
6th Floor
Chicago
Illinois 60601

Space/Management Programs
200 E. Randolph Drive
Suite 6907
Chicago
Illinois 60601

312.263.6605
312.263.1228 (Fax)
www.ghk.net

New York
Boston
Baltimore
Washington, DC
San Francisco

Griswold, Heckel & Kelly Associates, Inc. and Space/Management Programs

High Impact Spaces
Chicago, Illinois, Florence, Kentucky and Cambridge, Massachusetts

Is your workplace fun? Our grandparents would find this question incomprehensible. Yet high-technology companies have done a profound favor to employees of organizations everywhere by demonstrating that the workplace can help attract and retain employees. Architects and interior designers have spent years trying to prove a causal link exists between workplace design and worker performance. Now, under pressure to recruit qualified people, high-technology businesses have seized on environmental design to make work more rewarding for workers. For example, Griswold, Heckel & Kelly Associates, Inc. and Space/Management Programs recently designed offices for three high-technology clients: DriveLogic in Chicago, Illinois, which needed a 17,000-square foot facility and Cinergy in Florence, Kentucky, which needed a 7,000-square foot trading floor and other spaces totaling 18,000 square feet, and NetVentures in Cambridge, Massachusetts, which needed a 5,050-square foot facility. All faced tight deadlines, stringent budgets, sophisticated technological demands and talented employees with high expectations—and all have gratefully reported that their new offices are far more than functional. In fact, they're fun.

Griswold, Heckel & Kelly Associates, Inc. and Space/Management Programs

Brown Brothers Harriman
Boston, Massachusetts

Old and venerable banking halls may be supported by the sturdy bone and muscle of oversized structure and durable architecture, but their organs—the vital mechanical, electrical and plumbing systems on which Internet age businesses increasingly depend—frequently need replacement. The respected investment banking house of Brown Brothers Harriman recognized this in retaining Griswold, Heckel & Kelly Associates to renovate and upgrade 35,884 square feet of space for 76 employees in its existing building in Boston's financial district. No one could improve on the superb period detailing adorning the banking hall, executive offices, private offices, open plan areas, conference rooms, dining room and kitchenettes. But the space required new building core systems— including a new sprinkler system with piping concealed behind elaborate plaster ceilings. Ironically, because of diligent restoration and reconstruction, Brown Brothers Harriman looks and works better now than it has in years.

Upper left: Board of Directors dining room.
Left: Conference room conceals video teleconferencing hardware in armoire.
Far left: Banking hall features floating conference center.
Opposite: Elevator lobby features grillwork from earlier elevators.
Photography:
Ed Jacobi.

Griswold, Heckel & Kelly Associates, Inc. and Space/Management Programs

Andersen
Chicago, Illinois

"My Kingdom," to paraphrase Shakespeare, "for a brand." Making brand identities visible in the divisions or affiliates of companies in multiple markets has become a concern across the globe. To renovate the business units in Andersen's 342,380-square foot, 11-floor facility in Chicago, Griswold, Heckel & Kelly Associates gave each unit's space an individual identity while adhering to corporate branding standards. The award-winning project has created interiors with open plan work stations, teaming rooms, hoteling areas, conference centers, private offices (relatively few), cafes and lunchrooms that are light, colorful and high in density with a minimum of circulation area. By emphasizing a "flattened hierarchy," flexibility and spontaneous meetings, the units of Andersen are off to a fine, fresh start.

Griswold, Heckel & Kelly Associates, Inc. and Space/Management Programs

Heller Financial
New York, New York

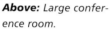
Above: Large conference room.
Right: Reception.
Below right: Private offices.
Photography: Cervin Robinson.

Corporate America's current emphasis on teamwork has stood the old spatial order of office design on its head. Consider the design of the newly renovated, 65,000-square foot, two-story office of Heller Financial in New York, designed by Griswold, Heckel & Kelly Associates. Its private offices have been reduced in size (10 feet x 10 feet) and relocated from the perimeter to the interior, the general office space has a new, clear view of the windows, executive offices are more modest at 10 feet x 15 feet each, and the facility's two conference rooms have become better equipped and more strategically situated at the reception area. Where's the focus in the new space? The conference rooms, appropriately enough, where clients are received.

Griswold, Heckel & Kelly Associates, Inc. and Space/Management Programs

Constellation Energy Source
Baltimore, Maryland

As California demonstrates, the deregulation of America's once-stodgy energy industry remains complex and unpredictable. A dynamic industry outpost recently opened in Baltimore, where Griswold, Heckel & Kelly Associates designed a 50,200-square foot office for Constellation Energy Source. The energy trading organization needed a workplace that quickly and economically responded to change, and attained its flexibility by adopting a universal module and furniture standard for private offices and open plan work stations, and equipping the trading room with infrastructure to expand positions rapidly from the initial 48 to a maximum of 110—which has happened. As anyone can see by looking from the executive visitors' area into the trading room, Constellation is very much "on."

Above: Executive visitors' area.
Below left: Trading room.
Below right: Executive boardroom.
Photography: Alain Jaramillo.

Godwin Associates

7000 Central Parkway
Suite 1020
Atlanta
Georgia 30328
770.804.1280
770.804.1284 (Fax)
www.godwinassociates.com

Godwin Associates

Security First Network Bank
Atlanta, Georgia

Left: *A cluster of collaboration spaces.*
Below: *Primary entrance.*
Opposite: *Interactive recreation area and breakroom.*
Photography: *Robert Thien/Robert Thien Photography.*

Security First Network Bank, termed the "Unbank Bank," presented a unique challenge to Godwin Associates in designing the Internet bank's 40,000-square foot corporate office for 260 employees in Atlanta. This subsidiary of an established Canadian banking institution intended to conduct all the standard operations of a bank. However, it wanted to do so in an environment that would be attractive to its young, growing workforce, encouraging interaction and creativity as part of an effort to enhance employee morale. Godwin Associates came up with an award-winning open plan office defined by working units clustered in "pods." "Destination points," stimulating spaces for both traditional and informal gatherings are located at four primary sites. Many other collaboration spaces, including private telephone enclave rooms and small soft seating rooms, are scattered throughout the facility.

Godwin Associates

Viewlocity
Atlanta, Georgia

First impressions of the Atlanta office for European-based Viewlocity can take visitors by surprise. The main entry of the 23,000-square foot facility designed by Godwin Associates for 100 employees looks intriguing and inviting, offering visual technology, interactive communication and displays of customer achievements, in a visual setting of comfortable lounge furnishings. The interior design evolved through a careful discovery process that involved Godwin Associates facilitation of strategic sessions with the American "founding group" of Viewlocity—with one of the outcomes being to make sure first impressions would be lasting ones. A principal goal for Viewlocity, a provider of supply chain management software for e-business, is indeed to make a powerful first impression on U.S. clients and venture capitalists. As you go beyond the entry, the flexible and dynamic environment of demountable partitions, open plan furniture systems, mobile furnishings and components, reveals its other goals of accommodating business and staff growth, and attracting and retaining employees.

Above: *Main entry.*
Left: *Main presentation room.*
Below left: *Touch down space.*
Below right: *Breakroom.*
Photography: *Robert Thien/Robert Thien Photography.*

Godwin Associates

Global Support Technology Center
Atlanta, Georgia

Left: *The 24/7 monitoring area.*
Right: *Corridor equipped for sales and marketing.*
Below left: *Customer viewing area.*
Photography: *Robert Thien/Robert Thien Photography (left), Brian Robbins/Robbins Photography, Inc. (right, below left).*

Many customers will never see the Global Support Technology Center in Atlanta that serves their technical needs. This fast-tracked 24/7 center is a source of technical support, and a marketing center of specialized products — a visual showcase for customer tours that is poised to handle confidential projects or crises whenever necessary. The 6,500-square foot facility, designed by Godwin Associates includes a computer lab, customer viewing area, demonstration area library and breakout meeting area. Close attention to operating issues by Godwin Associates enables the operating staff to eliminate customer viewing capabilities the moment sensitive matters arise by use of mechanized privacy screens. Information regarding a customer's equipment can be transferred to an engineering customer crisis room as soon as a problem is detected, allowing for quick and concise problem solving.

Godwin Associates

DeKalb Office Environments
Alpharetta, Georgia

Organizations commonly outgrow their environments. However, the recent impact of business change on DeKalb Office Environments, a highly charged, well integrated and widely respected furniture dealership in Alpharetta, Georgia, was anything but ordinary. When Godwin Associates was retained to design a new, 35,000-square foot facility for DeKalb, it

related to the dealership from a company-to-company perspective, rather than the traditional design-firm-to-design-client relationship. Partnering with DeKalb to bring its vision to reality, Godwin Associates introduced the concept of a furniture dealership as a virtual working laboratory to study the evolving workplace of offices today. The award-win-

ning design establishes conceptualized, interactive vignettes to highlight problem solving through design. Blending the right furniture, finishes, lighting design and graphic elements, the vignettes allow DeKalb to produce finely detailed, yet easily changeable solutions to its customers' specific design problems. The design formulates self-sufficient working com-

Left: Main entry with side-to-side portals.
Above: Private offices and collaborative meeting space of demountable partitions.
Top: Interactive cafe.
Opposite: Satellite collaboration area and coffee bar.
Photography: Robert Thien/Robert Thien Photography.

Right: Primary break-room area.
Far right: Architectural soffit and carpet as wayfinding tools.
Below: Executive suite.

munities that group complementary products from Steelcase and/or Steelcase Design Partnership companies. The cumulative effect of these innovative ideas is to transform the various functioning elements of DeKalb, including the executive suite, open plan office area, main training facility, collaboration/cafe lounge area, informal/soft seating meeting areas, cafe, meeting kiosk/coffee bar area and telephone enclaves, into a working, interactive extension of the real world outside the dealership's walls— all providing solutions that customers trust to perform just as well in their own environments.

Group Goetz Architects

2000 L Street, NW
Suite 410
Washington DC 20036   Reston
202.682.0700   New York
202.682.0738 (Fax)   Los Angeles
www.gga.com   London
info@gga.com   Bogotá

Group Goetz Architects

1307 New York Avenue
Washington, D.C.

Left: *Multipurpose room for over 100 people.*
Below left: *Boardroom.*
Below right: *View of main lobby.*
Opposite: *Lobby with elevators and attendant desk.*
Photography: *Maxwell MacKenzie.*

Four higher education associations have dramatically demonstrated that there really is strength in unity by forming an unusual joint venture to purchase and redevelop 1307 New York Avenue, a 105,000-square foot building in downtown Washington, D.C. With industrial revenue bond financing, a real estate tax exemption and the design services of Group Goetz Architects, the associations created a coherently designed building to cut occupancy costs, provide space for frequent and varied meetings, and enhance employee productivity and morale—while projecting an image of higher education as a benefit to society that would be legible to current and potential members, existing and future employees and the public. In addition to designing the floors for the individual associations, the architect designed the public spaces that project a unified identity for the associations, including reception area and ante room, boardroom, conference room and multipurpose room seating over 100 people. The handsome, economical and versatile facility confirms, in the management committee's words, that "being non-profit is non-limiting."

Group Goetz Architects

Circle.com
Baltimore, Maryland

Left: Conference room with translucent layering.
Right: Reception area.
Bottom opposite: View of glass fronted conference room.
Photography: Ron Solomon.

The energy level is high at Circle.com, and the 7,000-square foot headquarters designed by Group Goetz Architects in Baltimore's Inner Harbor expresses it. A marketing company specializing in strategic Internet consulting for Fortune 1000 companies and other prestigious clients, Circle.com houses some two dozen people in general marketing, account management, concept, design and production within a "sleek, chic and dynamic" interior quite unlike its parent company in the same building. The new facility makes traditional and modern materials, including limestone, glass and mechanical shade scrim stretched between aircraft cable, appear to float in a dynamic setting of luminous space. What better vantage point is there to chart the future of Internet business?

Group Goetz Architects

Lucent Technologies
Washington, D.C.

Right: *State-of-the-art presentation area.*
Below: *A corridor and multi-media gallery.*
Opposite: *Staircase from reception to cafe.*
Photography: *Paul Warchol.*

Because Washington, D.C. is an old Southern city of conservative taste, the new 80,000-square foot headquarters for the Government Solutions group of Lucent Technologies, designed by Group Goetz Architects, is daring in more ways than one. The relocation of two suburban divisions and an outlying metropolitan one to the heart of the capital, close to U.S. government customers, by the president of Government Solutions was bold enough. However, rather than hew to the standard office interiors favored by many federal vendors, the company built a workplace to evoke the excitement of the communications revolution. The flexible and ergonomic work space is a showcase for technology in an optimal, networked setting, offering such amenities as a cafe, forum and team rooms. Communications can chart its future here.

Group Goetz Architects

World Bank InfoShop
Washington, D.C.

If the boundaries between bookstores, libraries and cafes have been successfully crossed in recent years then the debut of the World Bank's 7,000-square foot InfoShop, designed by Group Goetz Architects, in Washington, D.C. should be equally well received. The World Bank decided to co-locate its bookstore and public information center in a retail space that would express its focus on sharing knowledge, current information and best practice experiences worldwide. InfoShop imposes two overlapping grids on its floor plan, one paralleling the avenue, the other introducing curved and angular elements, and uses custom designed bookshelves and other display fixtures to tell visitors where everything is, just as any good bookstore or library does.

Right: *Custom designed display fixtures.*
Below: *Interior at entry.*
Photography: *Maxwell MacKenzie.*

H. Hendy Associates

2415 Campus Drive
Suite 110
Irvine
California 92612
714.851.3080
714.851.0807 (Fax)
www.hhendy.com

H. Hendy Associates

eHomes.com
Aliso Viejo, California

Above: *3-D computer model of design.*
Right: *View through actual storefront.*
Below right: *Expresso bar.*
Opposite: *Interior with kiosks.*
Photography: *Paul Bielenberg.*

You say you still haven't bought a home online? As a pioneer in online residential real estate services in southern California, Aliso Viejo-based eHomes.com is readying a clicks-and-mortar strategy of nationwide Web services. It will be supplemented by a roll-out of retail sites staffed by real agents and equipped with Internet-linked kiosks for browsing. To enter the retail business, eHomes.com commissioned H. Hendy Associates to design a prototype store with a feeling of domestic warmth and Internet sophistication, a space plan encompassing semi-private meeting rooms, an agent hoteling area, children's play space, espresso bar, Internet kiosks, and a highly visible signage program, all on just 2,200 square feet. The computer modeling of the store design was so accurate and satisfying that eHomes.com has given the design firm additional work.

H. Hendy Associates

buy.com
Aliso Viejo, California

When Scott Blum, founder of buy.com, a leading online retailer with 12 specialty stores serving 3 million customers that calls itself the "Internet Superstore," spoke out at the kick-off meeting to develop a new, 52,000-square foot headquarters in Aliso Viejo, California, he asked H. Hendy Associates for a design of "simplicity, flexibility, quality."

Buy.com got it—along with a central core system of space planning that supports technical operations with a satellite computer file server room, an A/V teleconferencing room and a high-tech plasma flat screen area, plus compact yet expandable work station standards and such amenities as a catered lunchroom, showers and on-demand food and beverage areas to sup-

port workers like the 24/7 customer service representatives you reach when you absolutely must shop at 2 a.m.

Above left: Full-service lunchroom.
Left: Reception area.
Below right: Seating in reception area.
Photography: Milroy & McAleer Photography.

H. Hendy Associates

An Energy Company
Chicago, Illinois

Deregulation has galvanized the once-sleepy power generation industry, making it more dynamic than ever before. Among the key players in the new marketplace is the energy company that commissioned H. Hendy Associates to design their two-story, 42,000-square foot regional headquarters in Chicago. The company (which owns nearly 23,000 megawatts of generat-ing capacity and interests in more than 75 power projects globally) enjoyed a long relationship with H. Hendy Associates prior to this installation. Consequently, they quickly identified key issues for housing the regional enterprise that the company had acquired. The goal was to create a functional and cost-effective environment that linked the company's identity with Chicago's cultural history. The successful solution, inspired by Frank Lloyd Wright's Prairie Style, is firmly rooted in the Midwest.

Left: *Reception area.*
Directly above: *Executive lounge.*
Above: *Boardroom vignette.*
Top: *Executive lounge.*
Opposite: *Boardroom.*
Photography: *Chris Barrett/Hedrich Blessing.*

H. Hendy Associates

Joe's Garage
Tustin, California

Here's the latest spin on car talk: The American Society of Mechanical Engineers recently declared the automobile "the greatest mechanical engineering achievement of the 20th century," ahead of the airplane, refrigeration, and the Apollo moon mission. Car mania is certainly driving "Joe's Garage," a 30,000-square foot car museum, special events facility and private office in Tustin, California, designed for businessman Joe MacPherson by H. Hendy Associates. To turn a collection of vintage cars into a viable business, MacPherson transformed a two-story parking structure into an entertainment venue using facades based on California period architecture, realistic murals depicting California history, and theatrical lighting. Chamber of Commerce meetings, art exhibitions and weddings confirm that Joe's Garage is now a hot spot—if you find parking.

Top left: *Gift shop cash wrap.*
Top right: *Gift shop and banquet hall.*
Above: *Museum floor.*
Photography: *Chris Barrett/Hedrich Blessing.*

Hillier

500 Alexander Park CN 23
Princeton
New Jersey 08543
609.452.8888
609.452.8332 (Fax)

www.hillier.com

New York
Newark
Philadelphia
Washington
Scranton
Kansas City
Dallas
London

AND 1
Paoli, Pennsylvania

Left: *Company retail store.*
Right: *"The Lane."*
Photography: *Jim Hedrich/Hedrich Blessing.*

Athletes are living proof that doing one thing well can yield powerful results. So it shouldn't be surprising when a non-traditional, high-energy, street-wise company declares, "AND 1 only does basketball." AND 1 simply wants to be the number one designer and manufacturer of basketball shoes and apparel in the world, and it recently retained Hillier to design its 40,000-square foot headquarters in Paoli, Pennsylvania to send this message. At the heart of its space is "The Lane," the main circulation corridor that begins in the reception area and terminates at the full-scale basketball court and cafe/lounge. It's surrounded by materials and finishes common in the urban environment, such as stained and sealed concrete floors, exposed structural systems and utilities beneath a 15-foot ceiling, sealed plywood and drywall partitions and work stations divided by chain-link fence panels. You better believe AND 1 likes this "aggressive fun."

Hillier

StarMedia
New York, New York

Left: Lounge.
Above: Open plan area.
Photography: Paul Warchol.

How likely are Latinos to visit StarMedia, one of the first online networks catering to them? Consider that the company has grown from six employees to over 400 and has had to build a new, 100,000-square foot headquarters, designed by Hillier. The versatile facility conveys the image of a dynamic

Right: *"Chat rooom."*
Lower right: *View outside "chat roooms."*

company with a visually oriented product, meets current needs of employees working amid an abundance of computer equipment, and provides for future growth by maintaining flexibility in furnishings and floor plans. Flexibility is paramount in the open plan interiors to let StarMedia quickly reconfigure its work stations to accommodate a changing work force, since the company has been hiring five or six new employees per week. Yet the design also provides an attractive and supportive environment for employees, and incorporates formal conference rooms and informal meeting areas in a variety of sizes and shapes, handsome contemporary furnishings and a dramatic lighting scheme to help them perform at their best.

Hillier

Pharmacia Corporation
Peapack, New Jersey

Left: *Executive waiting area.*
Right: *Work lounge.*
Below: *Servery.*
Opposite: *Main lobby.*
Photography: *Barry Halkin.*

Quality endures. An eloquent testimonial to doing things right is the 10-building, 450,000-square foot corporate campus originally designed by Hillier for Beneficial Management Corporation—now redesigned by Hillier as the world headquarters of Pharmacia Corporation, a recognized leader among the world's pharmaceutical companies in such therapeutic areas as arthritis/inflammation, antibiotics, oncology and ophthalmology. Though the well-preserved exteriors needed no changes, the interiors were completely remodeled to create a contemporary work environment, meet advanced technology needs and reflect Pharmacia's corporate culture. Seventy-five percent of the work spaces are private offices located primarily in the interior of the building, so that the perimeter can be used for circulation and daylight. Education and interaction are promoted through a state-of-the-art conference and training center as well as extensive video conferencing facilities, training rooms and work lounges with connectivity. Employees' personal needs are addressed through amenities including the dining room and servery, fitness center and company store. Pharmacia's new home is both timely and timeless.

Turkiye Is Bankasi A.S.
Istanbul, Turkey

Below: *Board room.*
Bottom: *Executive reception hall.*
Right: *Banking hall.*
Photography: *Paul Warchol.*

Despite the fact that Turkiye Is Bankasi A.S. was established at the close of the Ottoman Empire by Kemal Ataturk, the father of modern Turkey, its contemporary and sophisticated new headquarters in Istanbul, designed by Hillier, avoids specific references to its rich heritage or that of its nation. The opening of the Bank's new facility completes its move from Ankara, the capital of Turkey, to the heart of the nation's business center. It clearly reflects a desire to look forward rather than backward in its banking hall, offices, trading floor, 800-seat theater, cafeteria and exhibition gallery—a choice that has produced impressive results.

HLW International LLP

115 Fifth Avenue
New York
New York 10003
212.353.4600
212.353.4666 (Fax)
www.hlw.com
sbartzke@hlw.com

HLW International LLP

Agency.com
New York, New York

Capturing eyeballs seems as much of a challenge for the new economy as for the old. For Agency.com, one of the largest and most successful Internet advertising agencies aiding clients in the eyeball sweepstakes, rapid growth in its New York office created a problem common to businesses everywhere. How do you house an expanding staff in 156,000 square feet of office space to reflect the identities of its work groups, yet support the activities and personalities of individual employees? The versatile open plan design produced by HLW International creates neighborhood centers for Agency.com's work groups, each equipped with a library, brainstorming room and other support functions. These centers, all interconnected by main circulation spines, act as fixed nuclei to express the culture of their groups, yet allow the overall planning of the facility to remain flexible. Seven floors of open plan offices, private offices, conference facilities, cafeteria and game room give Agency.com's employees a sympathetic environment in which their clients' market share can only grow.

Above left: Team Room.
Above right: Reception with award display wall.
Left: Interconnecting stair with conference area beyond.
Opposite: Zen Den.
Photography: Christopher Lovi.

HLW International LLP

Bernard Hodes
Venice, California

Left: General office space.
Below left: Main circulation corridor.
Opposite: Skylit area.
Photography: Benny Chan.

To work in a subterranean space means to work without windows, and anyone who designs an underground facility soon confronts the need to introduce natural light or simulated natural light below grade. This was the situation faced by the Bernard Hodes advertising agency in retaining HLW International to design its 13,600 square foot office on a single floor in Venice, California. The building to be occupied, Frank Gehry's famous "Binocular Building," developed to house another advertising agency, was no ordinary commercial space, to be sure. Yet there were skylights only above the ends of the space, leaving the interior decidedly in the dark. What HLW International has done is to blanket the open plan environment in bright, saturated colors, clean, modern furnishings, and a variety of lighting schemes that turn the ceiling into a luminous surface for direct and indirect light from soffits, pendant fixtures and the like. So the employees of Bernard Hodes remain underground, but they don't have to believe it, if they don't want to.

HLW International LLP

Fox Executive Building
Los Angeles, California

Above: *Main lobby.*
Below left: *Waiting area.*
Below right: *Boardroom.*

Sets aren't the only physical properties that the entertainment industry sets up and breaks down quickly. The production teams that create television programs and feature films often assemble their people and resources around them as needed only to release them once they have fulfilled their contracts. Consequently, television networks and movie studios house administrative operations in offices that are functional, cost-effective and easily reconfigured. The 195,000-square foot Fox Executive Building in Los Angeles, designed by HLW International, exemplifies this kind of facility. However, it has given the architect a rare opportunity to provide more than interior design for a client in need of office space. Here, the client also requested master planning for Fox Lot, the site of the office, the building housing the office, landscaping and graph-

ics. Because of this intensive involvement by HLW International, Fox Inc. has a property where the offices, arranged as a linear series of suites, and supporting spaces such as reception, conference facilities and screening rooms, all flow from a single functional and aesthetic vision—a unique property even in the entertainment industry.

Opposite:
Interconnecting stair at entry facade.
Below: *Supergraphics as wayfinding device in Fox Lot.*
Supergraphics: *Douglas Slone.*
Photography: *Milroy & McAleer.*

HLW International LLP

Accenture
Seoul, Korea

Above left: *Cafe.*
Above right: *Reception.*
Below left: *View from elevator lobby.*
Photography: *Tae-Ho Jung.*

The birth of the global economy has been driven by border crossings of businesses eager to market their products to consumers and other businesses in foreign lands. Along with U.S. companies in manufacturing, finance and entertainment, management consultants are being welcomed overseas, and the new, 35,000-square foot office for Accenture (formerly Andersen Consulting) is an intriguing example of this trend. The open team spaces, enclosed collaborative rooms, training rooms, touchdown spaces, focus rooms, private offices and cafe are part of a hoteling system with no assigned spaces that is new to Korea. Yet visitors will be quickly put at ease. Inside the modern interiors they will encounter elegant, comfortable furnishings and plenty of natural light to find their way within the global economy.

Hnedak Bobo Group

104 South Front
Memphis
Tennessee 38103
901.525.2557
901.525.2570 (Fax)
www.hbginc.com

3960 Howard Hughes Parkway
Suite 460
Las Vegas
Nevada 89109
702.948.2557
702.948.2558 (Fax)

Hnedak Bobo Group

Promus Hotel Corporation
Marketing Services Center
Tampa, Florida

Where do high energy and relaxation happily co-exist in the business world? A likely place to look is today's call center, a facility developed to help telemarketing personnel work at optimum levels for sustained intervals. A good example of what a modern call center can offer is the 24,000-square foot Marketing Services Center for 180 workers of Promus Hotel Corporation in Tampa, Florida, designed by Hnedak Bobo Group. The 24-hour call center's environment, which encompasses general administrative offices, call floor, breakroom, training facility and library, supports the work force through demanding hours of work and officially sanctioned time-off for rest. Among its numerous creative design concepts are an open floor plan of undulating walls splashed with vibrant primary colors, a lay-in ceiling that tilts in alternating directions within the tall structural bays for more openness and enhanced acoustics, and exposed building systems that act as primary visual elements. It's not your everyday workplace, for sure.

Top: *Breakroom.*
Above: *Reception desk area.*
Left: *Call center interior.*
Right: *Corridor and adjacent workspaces.*
Photography: *Jeffrey Jacobs.*

Hnedak Bobo Group

Union Planters Bank Headquarters
Memphis, Tennessee

Above: Teller area.
Left: Customer service and waiting areas.
Below: Executive board room.
Opposite: Gated entry to lobby.
Photography: Jeffrey Jacobs.

Tradition remains vital to the South at the dawn of the 21st century. Accordingly, the new, 83,000-square foot, five-story headquarters of Union Planters Bank in Memphis, Tennessee, has been designed by Hnedak Bobo Group to communicate permanence, stability and tradition to the customer while incorporating the latest in banking technology. The award-winning facility provides general administrative offices, executive offices, conference rooms and a customer service area for 170 bank employees and their customers in an impressive environment that recalls the neoclassical, Greek Revival architecture of turn-of-the-century Southern banking institutions. When asked about the eye-catching design, Ken Plunk, former president of Union Planters replied, "We just told the architect to come up with a building that looked like how a bank is supposed to look."

Hnedak Bobo Group

iXL Corporate Offices
Memphis, Tennessee

Prepare yourself to step inside the Internet. Though we may never inhabit physical space in the same way we explore an animated Web page, iXL Corporation's 25,000-square foot headquarters in Memphis,

Tennessee, designed by Hnedak Bobo Group, comes delightfully close. The office mimics the interactive Web sites that the dot-com designer creates for its clients. In fact, each of four distinct operations has its own unique, interactive

workplace to nurture creativity and efficiency. Thus, every space—from the executive offices, general administrative offices and presentation rooms to the creative department, computer programming depart-ment,, reception area

and "touchdown" spaces where visitors can plug in laptops—is equipped for intense, interactive use. To give the predom-inantly open setting its distinctive character, there are such unique finishing touches as curved walls in contrast-

ing blue, red, purple and yellow colors, cork floors, brushed steel panels, "buffalo-hair" carpet tiles and exposed wiring. Are you ready for your walk through cyberspace?

Opposite above: Lobby with kiosks.
Opposite left: Conference room view from hallway.
Above: Breakroom with pool table.
Right: Work stations.
Bottom right: Private editing room.
Photography: Jeffrey Jacobs.

Hnedak Bobo Group

Andersen Regional Offices
Memphis, Tennessee

Right: Hallway to offices.
Lower right: Private office with glass wall.
Bottom right: Lobby.
Below left: Elevator lobby.
Photography: Jeffrey Jacobs.

Because rules are sometimes meant to be bent, Hnedak Bobo Group was asked by Andersen (formerly Arthur Andersen) to merge their slick, contemporary corporate design standards with a more stately time-honored style befitting this Southern office and its regional clientele. Bending those rules, HBG took the current Andersen national standard and gave it a lesson in history and a twist on tradition. The 30,000-square foot, one and one half floor facility for 120 employees weaves together sleek interior glass, polished marble flooring and rich woods, acknowledging the sense of tradition found within the general accounting and consulting offices. And, their clients aren't the only ones who had an influence on the design. The interior office environment characterized by a mixture of glassed offices and open workspaces were clearly designed with the Andersen employee in mind.

Huntsman Architectural Group

50 California Street
Suite 700
San Francisco
California 94111
415.394.1212
415.394.1222 (Fax)
www.huntsmanag.com

Huntsman Architectural Group

Scudder Weisel Capital
San Francisco, California

Being the younger and more hip division of a successful, traditional investment organization, Scudder Weisel Capital needed to establish a setting of endurance, dependability and trust in wealth management for clients even as it continued to foster an entrepreneurial work environment for employees. Thus, Huntsman Architectural Group has conceived the 8,100-square foot San Francisco headquarters for 37 employees as essentially one large, open, interactive room with private, glass-fronted interior offices along one side and terraces and views along the other, all appointed in a classic, modern aesthetic that features fine furniture designed by Mies van der Rohe and Charles and Ray Eames. The various facilities, which include reception, multi-media board room, executive offices, private offices, open plan work stations, conference rooms and support spaces, are carefully designed to provide clients and employees appropriate surroundings, including dramatic views of the City by the Bay that everyone can enjoy.

Above left: Circular multi-media board room.
Above right: Executive office.
Left: Private office.
Opposite: Reception.
Photography: David Wakely Photography.

Huntsman Architectural Group

Actuate Corporation
South San Francisco, California

Above left: Conference room.
Above right: Reception area with conference rooms behind.
Right: General office area.
Photography: David Wakely Photography.

Life represents varying probabilities of risk in the actuarial business, so it was only natural for Actuate Corporation, an eight-year-old developer of actuarial software for large corporations, to want its 120,000-square foot offices on four floors in South San Francisco to project a visual impression of stability and innovation to visitors and 650 employees alike. Huntsman Architectural Group responded by designing the private offices, open plan work stations, conferencing center, corporate training center, employee lounges and network server facilities in a modern vision influenced by Asian motifs. To encourage employee interaction, the typical large floor plate is anchored by a continuous, street-like circulation path, illuminated by custom light poles that carry power and data services from the ceiling to the work stations, and enlivened by informal coffee and meeting areas where it's very probable Actuate's people will be gathering.

Huntsman Architectural Group   Sofinnova Ventures
San Francisco, California

Can a venture capital firm be properly housed in an industrial warehouse with a downtown San Francisco address? No problem. Venture capital firms have come a long way in the information age. In amassing prodigious amounts of funding for start-up ventures and preparing scores of entrepreneurs for initial public offerings, "VCs" have played an indispensable role in nurturing high technology that predates the commercial development of the Internet. Not surprisingly, they now mirror some of the cultural traits of the youthful enterprises they serve, including a preference for the iconic birthplace of start-ups in Silicon Valley and its offshoots: the garage. The venture capital firm of Sofinnova Ventures certainly had such an environment in mind when it retained Huntsman Architectural Group to design a 4,400-square foot space for eight employees. The space chosen to shelter the firm was a seismically retrofitted brick-and-terra-cotta penthouse with 20-foot high ceilings and panoramic views.

Above: Conference room.
Right: Private offices.
Opposite: Reception.
Photography: David Wakely Photography.

198

Paying homage to the garage, the venture capitalists and the architects decided that the space would be kept as open and naturally lighted as possible—even though the program called for multiple private offices and other enclosed spaces. To make these seemingly contradictory goals possible, the architects took advantage of the transparency and strength of polycarbonate panels to enclose volumes framed by exposed structural steel, producing private offices with full-height walls and defining an office zone that is perceived by visitors as a crystalline light box. Beyond this shimmering volume, visitors are delighted to enter the conference room and find themselves admiring magnificent views of San Francisco that would be the pride of any "garage."

Above: *Private office.*
Left: *Open plan office area.*

IA, Interior Architects Inc.

Atlanta
Boston
Chicago
Costa Mesa
Dallas
Denver
Ft. Lauderdale
Hong Kong
London
350 California Street   Los Angeles
Suite 1500   Miami
San Francisco   New Jersey
California 94104   New York
415.434.3305   Philadelphia
415.434.0330 (Fax)   Seattle
www.ia-global.com   Silicon Valley
corp.contact@ia-global.com Washington, DC

IA, Interior Architects Inc.

TiVo
San Jose, California

Frustrated by your VCR? TiVo, the San Jose, California-based provider of "personal television services" can power digital video recorders and work with every TV system—cable, digital cable, satellite, antenna, or combinations—to give viewers complete control over live TV, using sophisticated "smart" software to automatically find and record their favorite programs so they can watch what they want, when they want. TiVo's claim to be "so easy everyone in the house can use it" so that "there's always something great on for everyone" is backed by an intriguing statistic: 96 percent of TiVo subscribers would recommend TiVo to others. Not surprisingly, the 127,000-square foot headquarters that houses TiVo's office, support and data center space on four floors in two buildings has been designed by IA to match the lively, forward-looking spirit of the organization.

Left: General office area.
Above: Seating area in reception.
Opposite: Reception with distinctive Montis seating.
Photography: Beatriz Coll, San Farncisco.

Below: *Town Center.*
Right: *Main circulation path and entrance to editing room.*

IA's project team worked closely with TiVo to develop a "Hollywood meets 'toon town'" scheme, drawing on TiVo's residential focus to develop appropriate elements throughout the workplace, including a TV sculpture and interactive kiosk in the main lobby and a residentially styled "Living Room" for customer demonstrations. Yet the facility also acknowledges the vital role of technology by highlighting the editing rooms that line the main circulation path, and the interactive and family-style environment that originally nurtured TiVo's business atmosphere by creating a gathering area known as the 'Town Center' to encourage communication and house weekly "all-hands" lunch hour meetings. And as a happy ending, what could be more appropriate than a fast-forward schedule that saw IA complete TiVo in just over 20 weeks?

IA, Interior Architects Inc.   BMC Software
San Jose, California

One of the world's largest independent software vendors with fiscal year 2000 revenues exceeding $1.7 billion, Houston-based BMC Software delivers a comprehensive Service Assurance™ strategy for e-business systems management that enhances the availability, performance and recoverability of companies' business-critical applications. Clients who arrive at BMC's two-building, 220,000-square foot facility, designed by IA on the Novell campus in San Jose, needn't look far for evidence of the company's capabilities. The private offices for all software engineers and staff, employee lounge/gathering areas, conference rooms, multiple computer labs, data center server room, and executive briefing and training center project the classic modern image of a high-tech organization that knows exactly what it's doing. The project's heart is the main presentation area, the "Center for Excellence."

Left: Reception.
Above: Center for Excellence.
Photography: Beatriz Coll, San Farncisco.

Here clients can see an overview of products and services in the "Executive Briefing Room," view products in action in the "Nerve Center," and test products in the "Usability Lab." By spending time here or in the Training Center, where personal training is available, BMC's clients experience a setting that makes Service Assurance unmistakably visible.

Above: *Employee lounge.*
Right: *Nerve Center.*

Interprise

13727 Noel Road
Suite 200
Dallas
Texas 75240
972.385.3991
972.960.2519 (Fax)
www.interprisedesign.com

Accenture
(Formerly Andersen Consulting)
Irving, Texas

Many households move into new homes with old furnishings, and it is not unusual for businesses and institutions to do likewise. For its 3-story, 60,000-square foot office housing 235 employees in the Las Colinas district of Irving, Texas, Andersen Consulting retained Interprise to design an environment that would accomplish two major objectives. First, to reflect the management consultant's stability and depth of experience, and second, to make the new interior work with existing furniture. Program requirements called for private offices, open plan work stations, conference and training facilities, video conferencing and lunchroom. Everything was brought to a harmonious whole through color, form and detailing so there would be no hiatus between new and old. Thus, employees and visitors see a space that looks fresh and seamless from floor to ceiling.

Above: Reception and main conference room.
Right: Corridor beyond reception area.
Photography: Jon Miller/Hedrich Blessing.

Interprise

BDO Seidman
Dallas, Texas

Who says the open plan office is dead? Some 25 years after the emergence of the open plan office, private offices abound in Silicon Valley. Still, the advantages of compact footprint, mechanical flexibility and easy customization keep open plan offices in demand. This is shown in the 30,000-square foot office designed by Interprise for BDO Seidman, a national accounting firm, in Dallas, Texas. Expecting tremendous staff growth and anxious to increase communication between practice groups, the firm made a major cultural and spatial shift by moving to the new facility. While 95 percent of the staff previously occupied private offices and the remaining five percent used open plan work stations, 99 percent—including general and managing partners—now sit in open plan office space, ready for whatever challenges the new century may offer.

Right: *Reception area.*
Below left: *Open plan work station.*
Below right: *Reception desk.*
Photography: *Jon Miller/Hedrich Blessing.*

211

Simple, basic telephone, television or Internet services have virtually disappeared as active players in communications and media scramble to form alliances with one another and cross-sell new products to their customers. Cox Communications had such new-economy opportunities in mind when it invited Interprise to develop a new concept for its customer payment locations in New Orleans to stimulate customer awareness of its premier services and Internet access. The completed 3,000-square foot prototype "premier store" is designed to guide customers through a space featuring interactive kiosks supplemented by other display fixtures and feature elements, all promoting the latest market campaigns and service offerings. Besides anchoring a retail roll-out, the prototype design includes numerous elements that can be readily adapted to existing payment centers. Either way, it's probably coming to a location near you.

Above: Interior of premier store concept.
Left: Detail of interactive kiosk.
Photography: Paul Schiefer.

Interprise

Heidrick & Struggles
Dallas, Texas

Wanted: Executive talent. Prosperity has generated a strong demand for executive talent that heightens the value of organizations like Heidrick & Struggles, a respected executive placement firm. Accordingly, the firm retained Interprise to design a 13,000-square foot office in Dallas where potential job candidates would feel comfortable in a home-like setting. A traditional image was established for the facility by combining timeless, opulent materials such as stone, hardwood and carpet with refined modern architectural detailing and elegant furniture in historic styles. The space was handled with such assurance that the unavoidably narrow reception area looks as substantial as everything else.

Right: Corridor.
Below: Reception area.
Photography: Jon Miller/Hedrich Blessing.

Interprise

Legend Airlines
Dallas, Texas

Airline deregulation may not benefit business travelers whose seats are cramped, flights are canceled or departures are delayed. Hence the intense interest in start-up airlines that declare their intent to succeed by improving travel conditions, such as Legend Airlines, which commissioned Interprise to develop the look of its new, 37,000-square foot Dallas terminal in conjunction with the project architect. Because Legend offers passengers executive-style service, the physical environment of its airport terminal, including ticketing, baggage claim, security, concourse, gates and restrooms reveals a distinctly high-profile image that reinforces its logo, branding and uniforms. In this manner, the airline can begin its service long before the flight. As weary travelers might note, it's about time.

Above: *View of terminal interior.*
Right: *Vignette with logo.*
Photography: *Paul Schiefer.*

214

Interprise   **McCann-Erickson**
Dallas, Texas

You can't just pay to be cool, as any teenager knows. On the other hand, advertising agencies take care not to sprint too far ahead of clients even when they work at the cutting edge of media. In the case of McCann-Erickson, when this international advertising agency enlisted Interprise to express its avant-garde capability, it chose to alter only the most visible parts of its Dallas office. The reception area, board room, break out space, design staff office and lunchroom were transformed using such trendy materials as corrugated sheet metal, fiberglass, exposed wood studs, stained concrete floors, industrial-type hardware and lighting, and stylized modern furniture. Interior design with attitude!

Above: *Board room entry.*
Right: *Reception area.*
Photography: *Paul Schiefer.*

Interprise

NCSC
Dallas, Texas

Right: Entry.
Below: Call center operations room.
Photography: Jon Miller/Hedrich Blessing.

Where do "800" calls go? To call centers, the 24/7 lifelines of businesses to customers, vast fields of customer service representatives that mushroomed in the 1990s. The 37,000-square foot National Customer Support Center in Dallas, designed by Interprise for Pagenet, is a fascinating example. To turn a former supermarket into a successful call center for 300 employees of this leading provider of wireless messaging and information services in North America, Interprise grouped open plan work stations around a central circulation path and raised command center, created an attractive environment of colorful architectural forms, and installed needed building systems. Call Pagenet and see.

JPC Architects

13201 Bel-Red Road
Bellevue
Washington 98005
425.641.9200
425.637.8200 (Fax)
www.jpcarchitects.com

JPC Architects   F5 Networks
Seattle, Washington

Above: "Communicating stair" at 3rd floor.
Left: 4th floor reception seating.
Below: Open meeting area seen from 4th floor.
Opposite: 4th floor reception.
Photography: Fred Housel

One of the benefits corporate America is offering to attract and retain employees is a superior work environment. Consider F5 Networks' new, four-floor, 87,286-square foot Seattle office, designed by JPC Architects. A pioneer in high availability and Internet traffic/content management founded in 1996, F5 employs over 500 employees to develop turnkey solutions for over 2500 clients that increase the availability and performance of Internet Protocol-based servers and network devices such as firewalls, routers and cache services. To consolidate F5's growing staff, JPC Architects created a colorful, high-tech space featuring curved and exposed ceilings, aluminum door framing, maple doors, contemporary and retro furnishings and views of Puget Sound's Elliott Bay. For savvy techies, the reception area was inspired by a cross section of a networking cable.

JPC Architects

Sirach Capital Management, Inc.
Seattle, Washington

"We strive to provide clients with nothing less than superior investment management services," declares Seattle based Sirach Capital Management. Sirach is an investment management firm that has served institutions and individual clients since 1970. The firm prides itself on being an active and focused investor in growth oriented securities, and investment grade fixed income securities. Sirach has worked with JPC Architects to develop a 17,022 square foot office that graciously welcomes clients to the trading rooms, board-room, high net worth suites, and other facilities. The design solution is a reflection of the natural beauty of the Northwest, and its regional prominence as a hub for commerce worldwide. Sirach's success is built on a foundation that includes a "sound investment philosophy, probing research, experience, discipline, and insight." Sirach's new office space confirms it's credo.

Above: *Boardroom with custom table.*
Right: *Reception with steel waterfall.*
Above right: *Reception from elevators.*
Photography: *Michael Hewes*

JPC Architects   Immersant, Inc.
Seattle, Washington

Below: View towards main conference room. **Bottom:** Private office. **Photography:** Douglas J. Scott.

Does an Internet consultant and developer that helps companies develop and refine Web initiatives belong in a loft within a historic timber structure on the waterfront? When JPC Architects helped Immersant, formerly Bowne Internet Solutions, move into Seattle's 61 Columbia Street on a limited budget, the design firm took advantage of both the technological nature of the business and the robust character of the building by exposing the heating, ventilation, cable and lighting equipment. Timber columns and beams became architectural elements, combined with slate, carpet, drywall and simple, utilitarian furnishings. As a result, the dynamic, two-story, 35,000-square foot space for 158 employees seems entirely appropriate for a demanding business, expressing an aesthetic of function that celebrates the playful blending of old and new.

JPC Architects

Barclay Dean
Construction Services
Bellevue, Washington

Right: Reception area featuring ventwood, stainless steel and MDF. *Below:* Corner of boardroom and video wall, highlighting use of steel, ventwood, limestone and carpet. *Photography:* Jeff Beck.

How does a builder build for itself? Bellevue, Washington-based Barclay Dean Construction Services, a general contractor established as a business in 1949 and incorporated as a "GC" in 1990, wanted its new office to demonstrate its expertise to clients in metropolitan Seattle. Barclay Dean retained JPC Architects to create an 11,879-square foot showcase of materials and methods to attest to its capabilities in such specialties as large retailing facilities, warehouses, office buildings, hotels and tenant improvement projects. The resulting space is a display of diversity spanning from utilitarian to high-tech. Metal panels, fiberboard, architectural glass, wood and other materials blend harmoniously in furnishing a reception area, boardroom, private offices and lunchroom.

Kallmann McKinnell & Wood Architects, Inc.

939 Boylston Street
Boston
Massachusetts 02115
617.267.0808
617.267.6999 (Fax)
www.kmwarch.com
info@kmwarch.com

Kallmann McKinnell & Wood Architects, Inc.

Do factories and offices mix? The two were linked at the dawn of the industrial age, although offices were rudimentary appendages until the challenges of sales overshadowed production. Yet fine examples of factories with offices are flourishing, such as the 167,000-square foot corporate headquarters of Arrow International, Reading, Pennsylvania, designed by Kallmann McKinnell & Wood Architects. This handsome and original structure for 250 employees includes reception, private offices, library, R&D laboratories, training center, engineering facilities, cafeteria, fitness—and a 24-hour manufacturing wing for the company's products, medical equipment—set on a 125-acre field. Combining these functions requires different architectural strategies, so the architect organ-

ized the floor plan as a series of parallel tracks housing the manufacturing and laboratories in one-story high spaces and the offices as a three-story high curving block overlooking the wooded landscape. Dramatic "indoor street"-style circulation corridors orient people to the various components of the facility, successfully conveying the tradition of factory and office into the 21st century.

Above left: *Exterior of offices.*
Above right: *Cafeteria dining room.*
Right: *Cafeteria serving line.*
Opposite: *Three-story atrium and suspended floors of offices.*
Photography: *Steve Rosenthal.*

Kallmann McKinnell & Wood
Architects, Inc.

Becton Dickinson & Company
Franklin Lakes, New Jersey

Try to visualize planting a 350,000-square foot corporate headquarters and a 450,000-square foot divisional headquarters for Becton Dickinson & Company in Franklin Lakes, New Jersey without disturbing the heavily wooded, 130-acre site. Sounds implausible? The remarkable complex designed by Kallmann McKinnell & Wood Architects displays the determination of a prominent provider of medical devices and health care systems and services and its architect to respect the beauty of the landscape while creating a superior workplace. Some 1,500 employees work in the private offices, open plan offices, conference rooms, laboratories, legal library, auditorium, cafeteria and fitness center. Building I houses the primary corporate administration functions while Building II serves divi-sional operations and laboratory R&D. But here conventional descriptions yield to an extraordinary, award-winning design. Both sensitively land-scaped buildings have finger-like, two- and three-story office wings that extend down the sloping terrain, giving occupants optimal views and daylight. A series of interior atria introduce what employees deep within the buildings experience as outdoor environments. Though a facility of this scope has inevitable consequences for its site and occu-pants, seldom have they seemed so rewarding.

Left: Large conference room.
Above left: Building II exterior.
Above right: private office.
Top right: Auditorium.
Opposite: Atrium.
Photography: Steve Rosenthal

Kallmann McKinnell & Wood
Architects, Inc.

Ewing Marion Kauffman Foundation
Kansas City, Missouri

Devastated by floods and reconfigured by the U.S. Corps of Engineers, a former residential neighborhood has been reclaimed for the civic life of Kansas City, Missouri—as the splendid new headquarters of a prominent Midwestern philanthropy, the Ewing Kauffman Foundation, with master planning and design by Kallmann McKinnell & Wood Architects. The facility combines 105,000 square feet of office space and 32,000 square feet of conference facilities in a two-story building surrounding an open-ended courtyard and pond, a fitting centerpiece for the foundation's 37-acre midtown site. Rather than ignore the history of its site, the building firmly implants itself in the landscape of the new storm water management basin, overlooking ponds to its east, a creek to its south, a Memorial Garden to its west and a Nature Center to its east. (The two latter features were designed by other firms.) Since the philanthropy's mission is to encourage communication to build communities, the facility has been envisioned as a composition of streets, building facades and a Town Square. The design's symbolism is

Above right: *Circular conference setting.*
Above left: *Octagonal conference setting.*
Top left: *Conference room.*
Left: *Private office.*
Lower left: *Library.*

expressed outside through an architectural vocabulary whose pitched copper roof and brick construction recall the former residential neighborhood as well as the founder's use of the basement of his home to start his pharmaceutical business. Inside, circulation corridors are shaped to suggest short streets and long avenues, specially detailed open plan work station panels and storage units represent exterior elevations and front doors, and public spaces combine their scale, lowered or "excavated" floors (echoing the excavated pond flanked by the building's two wings) and major intersections of circulation paths to project the ambiance of outdoor plazas. Community-building communications will surely thrive here.

Keiser Associates, Inc.

419 Park Avenue South
New York
New York 10016
212.213.4500
212.213.6623 (Fax)
info@keiserassociates.com

Keiser Associates, Inc.

A Financial Institution
New York, New York

Throughout the 20th century, the financial world appointed its offices in furnishings created in enduring historical styles, drawing principally from the English and American 18th and 19th century canon. It's easy to understand the attraction, given the image of tradition, stability and sophistication projected by furniture, textiles, rugs, lighting and accessories inspired by the Queen Anne, Chippendale or Federal periods. The practice continues in the 21st century at the request of organizations such as the Financial Institution whose Manhattan office appears here, designed by Keiser Associates. Yet modernity has its place, particularly where finance meets high technology. The Financial Institution needed a self-contained conference center featuring state-of-the-art video conferencing for 45 people. The successful design solution includes reception, pre-function, food service with warming pantry, broker telephone area and guest toilets, and combines fine millwork and cabinetry and advanced electronics to produce the best of both worlds.

Above: Reception.
Opposite, above left: Guest restroom.
Opposite, above right: Pre function area.
Opposite, below: Conference room.
Photography: Max Hilaire.

Keiser Associates, Inc.

Morgan, Lewis & Bockius, LLP
Conference Center
New York, New York

Right: Conference room.
Below left: Reception.
Below right: Support services desk.
Photography: Max Hilaire.

The growing importance of conference centers, now served by an expanding array of information technologies, is establishing new priorities for major law firms around the nation. For the firm of Morgan, Lewis & Bockius in New York, its need for such a facility, a series of conference rooms of varying capacity for over 100 people that are served by ancillary facilities offering computers, printers, facsimile machines, copiers and support personnel, prompted it to retain Keiser Associates to design the complex within its existing office space. Having everything needed to conduct major negotiations and closing transactions is not only more efficient for all participants, it isolates the conference center's activities from the ongoing work of the firm, avoiding any inconvenience or additional stress at those moments when the stakes are particularly high.

Keiser Associates, Inc.

Jenkins & Gilchrist Parker Chapin, LLP
New York, New York

For a brief, enchanted moment, the Chrysler Building, designed by William van Alen and completed in 1930, reigned as the world's tallest skyscraper at 1,046 feet above midtown Manhattan. Though many other buildings subsequently shot past that elevation to claim and then lose the title, few have ever achieved the visibility of van Alen's wondrous Art Deco creation. Like other skyscrapers that preceded the triumph of the International Style in America, the Chrysler Building had a distinct form, including base, shaft and capital, with a spire that was unlike any other before or after it. Little wonder that when the law firm of Jenkins & Gilchrist Parker Chapin recently asked Keiser Associates to design its

Above: Reception.
Right: Waiting area.
Opposite: Elevator lobby.
Photography: Peter Paige.

110,000-square foot space in the building, the Keiser Associates recommended a facility that emulated the Art Deco era without attempting to copy the style or reproduce the building itself. The designers created the private offices, administrative support areas, library, conference center and lunchroom in a contemporary image that pays homage to the architectural masterpiece while looking to the future. The three-level environment is timely in its operations as well, weaving modern building mechanical and electrical systems through the seven decade-old structure without marring its appearance. Housed in this sophisticated workplace, Jenkins & Gilchrist Parker Chapin has every reason to believe it's on top of the world.

Above: *Internal staircase.*
Left: *Dining/conference room.*

240

Leotta Designers Inc.

601 Brickell Key Drive
Suite 602
Miami
Florida 33131
305.371.4949
305.371.2844 (Fax)
www.leottadesigners.com
johnke@leottadesigners.com

Leotta Designers Inc.

Walt Disney Television International-Latin America Coral Gables, Florida

As one of the world's top entertainment businesses, the Walt Disney Company knows how to get the most design services for its time and money, and its expertise is abundantly visible in the new, 28,840-square foot, 2-story space for 100 plus employees of Walt Disney Television International-Latin America, its Coral Gables, Florida-based TV headquarters and post production studio, designed by Leotta Designers Inc. The project's primary challenge was to include a media production facility with exacting acoustical requirements alongside private and open plan offices, training and meeting rooms, design studio and lunchroom. The solution was to place post production in a centralized location surrounded by "corner villages" containing other office functions. What grabs everyone's attention, however, are the vivacious yet inexpensive ways drywall, lighting and color honor Walt Disney's gift for creating a world of magic.

Top: General office area.
Above: Reception.
Left: Meeting room.
Opposite: Main hallway.
Photography: Nancy Robinson Watson.

Leotta Designers Inc.

American Airlines
Flagship Lounge
Miami, Florida

In a continuing effort to accommodate first-class passengers and enhance American Airlines' premium product, American Airlines has given the VIP customers a delightful incentive to choose its flights—the 3,400-square foot American Airlines Flagship Lounge at Miami International Airport, designed by Leotta Designers Inc. This facility, designed for 50 customers, will be rolled out worldwide to make waiting for first-class transcontinental and international flights as refreshing and productive as possible. To create a club-like setting that embodies the utility, comfort and elegance American wants to project, the design firm has produced a unique facility incorporating a clever geometric floor plan that looks much larger than it is, fine building materials and furnishings in stylish colors and finishes that will repay their cost with durability, local art that imparts the exotic flavor of Miami's diverse cultural roots, and such appealing amenities as the check-in reception, lounge, food service area, kitchen, showers, washrooms and valet service. The airline's senior officers have already proclaimed the Flagship Lounge as one of their finest clubs. Guess how you'll book your next flight.

Top: Lounge.
Opposite: Check-in reception.
Right: Glass alcove divides in lounge.
Photography: Nancy Robinson Watson.

Leotta Designers Inc.

Xerox
Stamford, Connecticut

Update. Make it better. Repeat when necessary. Business interiors are seldom permanent. However, the relationships between corporate clients and interior designers can be very enduring, as illustrated by Xerox Corporation's 15-year association with Leotta Designers Inc. in maintaining the 255,000-square foot corporate headquarters that shelters some 600 employees in Stamford, Connecticut. Remodeling a large and complex existing facility differs considerably from building a comparable space from scratch, since the premises remain occupied by the work force during construction, incremental alterations tend to complement existing elements, and the construction's environmental side effects must be isolated to minimize disruptions to the daily operations. Doing all this while sustaining a relationship with Xerox senior management has been the responsibility of the principals and staff of Leotta Designers for over 15 years at the office copier and information systems giant. The long-term ties have been mutually beneficial.

Above left: Executive office.
Above right: Boardroom.
Right: Main hallway off lobby.
Opposite: Atrium cafeteria.
Photography: Peter Paige.

Xerox relies on services from a trusted design firm that comprehends its corporate culture, operating procedures, timetables and budgets. Leotta Designers provides a steady flow of programming, space planning, design, construction documents and construction administration services to a major corporate client—and is present to gauge the impact of these services. Recent assignments have involved the revision and updating of numerous strategic spaces, the video conference center and the atrium cafeteria and lobby. At the dawn of the Internet era, the ties between Xerox and Leotta Designers seem strong, nurtured by the designer's close attention and the client's ongoing thanks.

Above: Training/conference facility.
Right: Executive conference room.

Lieber Cooper Associates

444 North Michigan Avenue
Suite 1200
Chicago
Illinois 60611
312.527.0800
312.527.3159 (Fax)
www.liebercooper.com
jason@liebercooper.com

Lieber Cooper Associates
Cassiday Schade & Gloor
Chicago, Illinois

Chicago's beloved Civic Opera House is also a distinguished but atypical office building, so when Cassiday Schade & Gloor retained Lieber Cooper Associates to design its 59,505-square foot office for 170 employees in this venerable structure, it faced numerous challenges. On a technological level, advanced HVAC, power, voice and data systems were needed that would go well beyond the building's unsophisticated infrastructure. On a spatial level, the building's square floorplate with a square atrium in the center created a continuous "race track" labyrinth until it was divided into quadrants with their own focal points. On an aesthetic level, the attorneys were concerned that vacating a modern structure for an older one might be misinterpreted as a step down by staff or clients. Lieber Cooper's airy, light and modern design dispels these concerns with warm colors, classic materials such as wood, stone and fabric, generous circulation and abundant daylight for the private offices, conference rooms, support and reception areas. Not surprisingly, the attorneys are now delighted to call the Civic Opera home.

Above: *View of reception area from elevator lobby.*
Right: *Reception area.*
Photography: *Scott McDonald/Hedrich Blessing.*

Lieber Cooper Associates

Lovells
Chicago, Illinois

Could there be a better showcase for a prominent London-based law firm's regional office in Chicago than the new, 20,500-square foot office designed by Lieber Cooper Associates for some 45 employees of Lovells (formerly Lovell White Durant) at the IBM Building? The IBM Building, an International Style masterpiece created by Ludwig Mies van der Rohe, provided an obvious source of inspiration for the classic modern environment of marble, maple wood and glass that Lovells has developed. This asset was enhanced by spectacular views down the Chicago River that are visible from 600 lineal feet of the office's 19th floor space. In addition, the attorneys contributed their impressive collection of contemporary art, inspiring the designers to create the gallery space that begins with a framed view of the lakefront from the elevator lobby that immediately expands in the reception area and envelopes the attorneys' offices, conference rooms, case rooms, library and lunchroom beyond. Yet the floor plan that Lieber Cooper has carefully crafted should not be overlooked either, since it takes advantage of an optimum window-to-building-core depth to achieve a key goal for Lovells, improving the "teaming" between attorneys and support staff. The success of this project is reflected in the 5,000-square foot extension that the designers are preparing for Lovells.

Left: Reception area viewed from elevator lobby.
Above: Corridor.
Opposite: Conference room entrance.
Photography: Marco Lorenzetti/Hedrich Blessing.

252

Lieber Cooper Associates

Piper Marbury Rudnick & Wolfe
Chicago, Illinois

Right: Corridor.
Below: Conference room.
Opposite: Communicating staircase.
Photography: Jon Miller/Hedrich Blessing.

What makes the 15-year relationship between the Chicago law firm of Piper Marbury Rudnick & Wolfe and the design firm of Lieber Cooper Associates so mutually rewarding is the profound involvement of the designers in the evolution of the law practice through the planning and design of its changing facilities. Beginning with the development of the original 164,000-square foot space for the firm of Rudnick & Wolfe in 1987, Lieber Cooper has become a strategic partner of the successor firm of Piper Marbury Rudnick & Wolfe, expanding the office to its current 216,872 square feet on eight floors in step with a work force that totals 672 employees today.

The forward-looking attorneys have challenged the designers to invent fresh ideas while retaining the original classic modern vocabulary, even as computers, information technology and economic forces continue to reshape the nature of practice. A pivotal moment in the relationship illustrates why the attorneys and designers are still working closely together today. At the seventh year of a 10-year lease commitment, Piper Marbury Rudnick & Wolfe requested Lieber Cooper's help in determining the cost of facility requirements for negotiating a long-term lease extension. Negotiations were completed successfully with a workletter allowance to

undertake the majority of work based on Lieber Cooper's cost projections, and the master planning performed during the facilitation process became a living, frequently-updated document that serves as the armature for quick responses to the law firm's additional space needs. Literally every aspect of the firm's classic modern environment, including attorneys' offices, conference rooms, support offices, case rooms, library, reception areas, lunchroom and highly visible communicating staircase, is the result of an ongoing assessment of where this dynamic organization stands in time and space.

LPA, Inc.

17848 Sky Park Circle
Irvine
California 92614
949.261.1001
949.260.1190 (Fax)
www.lpainc.com

LPA, Inc.

Woodbridge Office Building
Irvine, California

Below: Central lounge area.
Photography: Adrian Velicescu.

Above: Recreation building kitchen.
Left: Rock climbing wall in recreation building.
Below left: Private office.
Below right: Open office area.

Being asked to develop a 15,000 square foot stand alone office building for a dynamic financial management company of 18 employees is a unique opportunity. Then being asked to add a 7,000 square foot sports recreational facility that boasts multiple rock climbing structures, a game room, full kitchen and a swimming pool and you have something truly special. The challenge of placing this campus in a planned community with stringent design guidelines only helped to define the opportunity. A large greenbelt connecting the recreation and office buildings bordered by a dry river basin provided the design team with a vocabulary of openness. Formal interior spaces framed in the transparency of a nature-inspired canvas helped create the juxtaposition of this dynamic environment.

Informal gathering spaces are clad in simple materials and rendered by the warmth of natural light. Glazed partitions and skylights illuminate the large volumes that support daily operations, while state of-the-art technology and security systems link this group seamlessly to its East Coast partnerships. Crafting this award winning solution in concert with the client's unique requirements, LPA applied its strengths in Architecture, Landscape Architecture, Interior Design and Furniture Management.

LPA, Inc.

California State University Chancellor's Office
Long Beach, California

As the headquarters for the largest university system in the United States, with 23 campuses statewide, The California State University desired to create an environment that would support internal administrative functions while providing an external communication component. The award winning 165,000 square foot six-story building is located on the harbor in Long Beach, with views of the Pacific Ocean shared by over 500 staff members. To accomplish this, the design team reversed traditional perimeter office environments by moving private offices to the core. This core defines the inland edge of the facility and supports acoustically sensitive activities, daily utilities and building functions. Bordered by a common circulation spine, staff members and building amenities are accessible floor to floor via a series of convenient stairs and traditional elevators. The warm open space appointed in natural materials and finishes reflects the state's diverse offerings while providing a timeless foundation of a public facility. The ground floor Conference Center consists of a variety of meeting spaces from trustees, and campus presidents to student representatives. With system-wide influence, this facility is equipped with state-of-the-art technology in order to link to audiences throughout the state. LPA utilized its talents in Architecture, Interior Design, Signage, Furniture Management and Landscape Architecture to create this seamless expression of leadership for the California State University system.

Above left: Building exterior.
Right: Conference center.
Photography: Timothy Hursley.

260

Left: *Private offices in the core.*
Far left: *Main lobby stair.*

LPA, Inc.

KIA Motors, USA
Irvine, California

Right: Reception.
Below: Main lobby.
Bottom: Office corridor.
Photography: Adrian
Velicescu.

Take a building that has endured remodelings over the years that left it a tangle of mismatched construction, give it a clearly definable purpose and fresh look, and you know what KIA Motors and its design firm, LPA, Inc., have achieved in developing a new, 150,000-square foot U.S. Corporate Headquarters in Irvine, California. The nondescript lobby was reshaped and refinished to present the company and a number of its cars at their best. At the front of the facility executive and sales functions are located near the lobby to provide easy access to visiting clients and vendors. Administrative functions are centrally located, while technical training for KIA Motors' network of dealers takes place towards the back of the facility. KIA has produced a home worthy of its cars.

LPA, Inc.

Newmeyer + Dillion
Newport Beach, California

Law firms, practicing in a venerable profession based on precedence, have yielded with varying degrees of enthusiasm to such modern forces as information technology while retaining as much of their tradition as possible. In moving to a 22,000-square foot state-of-the-art facility for 85 employees designed by LPA Inc., in Newport Beach, California, Newmeyer + Dillion wanted to bring along certain aspects and components of its previous home. LPA helped its client identify these key components, which included fixtures and furniture, and incorporated into a fresh interior design. The space features private offices on the building perimeter, clerestory windows to bring daylight into interior offices, custom cherry work stations for secretaries, conference rooms, break room, law library, storage, satellite copy/printer areas, ancillary reading areas and lobby. As for the attorneys' response to the new facility, "...Our clients' response to the new office design has been tremendous. We will call on LPA to design our next space, and our next..."

Above left: Lobby.
Above right: Library and reading area.
Below right: Private offices and conference rooms.
Photography: Adrian Velicescu.

LPA, Inc.

Automobile Manufacturer
Torrance, California

Getting employees to think creatively is more easily accomplished in an environment that inspires the creative process. To develop such a space, an automobile manufacturer retained LPA, Inc. to convert a vehicle maintenance facility into a dynamic, flexible, and creative environment for a business unit established to pursue innovative ideas. Though the building was compact and windowless with high bay ceilings, LPA combined skylights, exposed ceilings, indirect lighting, and modular furniture to produce spaces that are bright, colorful, and open. LPA designed a staff teaming area dedicated to a more casual environment with lounge chairs and trade publications. This space is connected to a private meeting room by a 16' pivot wall that opens the space for large presentations. particularly captivating is the use of the open road as a metaphor to give the facility character. Complete with billboards" that line the edge of the "street" and a "gas pump" which houses supplies, this creative office provides the inspiration for its employees to think outside the box.

Mancini·Duffy

39 West 13th Street
New York, NY 10011
212.938.1260
800.298.0868
212.938.1267 (Fax)
www.manciniduffy.com
info@manciniduffy.com

Washington, DC
Mountain Lakes
San Francisco
Stamford

Mancini•Duffy

Condé Nast Publications
New York, New York

Above: Executive corridor.
Right: Art studio.
Below: Conference room exterior.
Opposite: Reception for Allure.
Photography: Peter Paige.

Print is alive and well. In fact, magazines are thriving in the Internet age. That's certainly true for one of the nation's most celebrated magazine publishers, Condé Nast, whose titles include *Vogue, The New Yorker, Architectural Digest, Vanity Fair* and *Glamour,* among others. A recent move by 2,000 employees has brought Condé Nast to a new, 760,000-square foot home designed by Mancini•Duffy in New York's Times Square.

Yet there is more involved here than a consolidation of dispersed operations, including the publisher's desire to let each magazine's space reflect its "brand," individual culture and style of working, and the commitment of the building's developer, Durst Organization, to use environmentally responsible building materials and systems. The private offices in the building's interior, open plan work stations on the perimeter, and con-

ference rooms, test and demonstration kitchens, auditorium, library, photo studio, cafeteria and private dining rooms show a Condé Nast that is ready for the millennium.

Mancini·Duffy

Prism Communication Services
New York, New York

Picture high-tech prodigies and B-school graduates getting along at work. It's one of numerous accomplishments within the new 45,000-square foot office designed by Mancini•Duffy for 250 employees of high-speed Internet access provider Prism Communication Services in New York. Among Prism's other program requirements were special facilities for presentations, demonstrations and other client-focused events, open general office areas, visi- ble back offices, such amenities as a café, town hall and meeting areas to encourage interaction among employees—on a layout that respected feng-shui principles. To make the environment within the century-old building easy to navigate, a serpentine circulation path links all public areas with its continuous hard ceiling, contrasting carpet inset, distinctive pendant lighting and curving glass walls. Furnishings are organically shaped yet functional, lighting is user- friendly, building systems are state-of-the-art, and the technicians and executives are working together as smoothly as the Internet access they provide.

Mancini•Duffy

BMC Software
Waltham, Massachusetts

Right: Customer lounge.
Below: Employee coffee bar.
Photography: Phillip Ennis.

Here's a timely example of the interesting pairings brokered by the information technology revolution: A showcase for corporate clients, open, inviting and corporate with a touch of high-tech flair, joined to a software research and development facility, cloistered, collegiate and comfortable for long hours of concentrated work. At BMC Software, Waltham, Massachusetts, the 175,000-square foot facility on two floors designed by Mancini•Duffy for 600 employees does indeed lead two separate lives—and shows it. The part that receives clients who attend training classes and demonstrations in briefing centers and dine in their own, reserved areas looks sleekly modern, while the remainder, featuring perimeter private offices, meeting areas with coffee bars, library and computer center, comes off as an informal, high-tech world in black, white and primary colors. Good people and good design pull everything together.

Mancini•Duffy

Internet Company
San Francisco, California

Anyone who has ever prepared dinner in 60 minutes or less knows what Mancini•Duffy faced in relocating this internet company. The assignment put 70 employees in a 10,000-square foot former health club and fitness center in San Francisco's Levi Plaza to establish a central location that could help recruit talent. Saving time and minimizing costs while projecting an upbeat, "start-up" feel meant retaining much of the existing construction and adapting it with stock materials, off-the-shelf furniture and various other products from local vendors who could deliver on a fast-track schedule. Since the space has limited natural light, conference areas, reception, lunchroom and other public functions cluster at the front, offices feed off a chalk-board-lined main corridor, and translucent fabric scrims reinforce privacy. Quick, inexpensive and functional.

Above left:
Chalkboard-lined corridor.
Above right: *Reception area.*
Photography:
Cesar Rubio/Cesar Rubio Photography.

Mancini·Duffy

Sports Illustrated
New York, New York

Like the final offensive drive before the clock halts a hotly contested game, the 165,000-square foot New York office of Sports Illustrated designed by Mancini•Duffy resembles a fast-moving target. The three-level facility that accommodates the magazine's 475 people has been created to respond quickly to changing business conditions with a "Flexible Work Environment," a universal infrastructure that supports all power, lighting, HVAC, data and telecommunications requirements, coupled with a "kit of parts" of interchangeable room partitions and work station components. However, as sports fans know, there's more to the game than technical prowess. The private offices, open plan areas, conference rooms, training and breakout areas, teaming lounges, reception and special accommodations for art, photography, imaging production and the like also represent a spirited celebration of sportsmanship in which the Sports Illustrated brand can be carefully managed season after season.

McCarthy Nordburg, Ltd.

3333 East Camelback Road
Suite 180
Phoenix
Arizona 85018.2323
602.955.4499
602.955.4599 (Fax)
main@mccarthynordburg.com
www.mccarthynordburg.com

McCarthy Nordburg, Ltd.

Cohen Kennedy Dowd & Quigley
Phoenix, Arizona

Having designed the original office for the law firm of Cohen Kennedy Dowd & Quigley, McCarthy Nordburg, Ltd. was pleased to design the new, 16,000-square foot home in Phoenix for its 22 employees. The partners requested an original design that would express the distinct personality and culture of their dynamic organization, and gave the designers considerable freedom to create the typical facilities of a law office and mock court room. The firm's extensive collection of contemporary art provided a springboard for the art gallery theme that pervades the entire environment, conveyed by crisp, contemporary architecture, neutral colors and dramatic lighting. The space's lively spirit can be seen even in the 125-foot long main corridor, a vibrant "art walk" that inspires employees and clients alike.

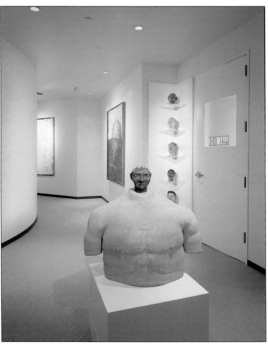

Above left: Conference room.
Far left: Entrance.
Left: Corridor.
Opposite: Reception.
Photography: Michael Norton.

McCarthy Nordburg, Ltd.

Gainey Village Health Club & Spa
Scottsdale, Arizona

Below: *Lobby.*
Photography: *Michael Norton.*

The largest facility of its kind in the Southwest, the 70,000-square foot Gainey Village Health Club & Spa in Scottsdale, Arizona features a full-service health club, a 25-room day spa and salon, and sports medicine and wellness center operated by Scottsdale Healthcare for an affluent clientele. The main challenge for McCarthy Nordburg, Ltd. as interior designer was to develop the chosen Ancient Native American theme in a sophisticated manner to harmonize with the building's contemporary architecture. The careful detailing is evident as soon as customers enter the lobby and view its inviting milieu of bold accent colors and stylish yet comfortable furnishings. A sense of welcome beckons throughout the facilities, so that even the locker rooms, appointed in Italian glass tile, maple wood lockers and stainless steel trim, provide an uplifting experience that customers want to return to again and again.

McCarthy Nordburg, Ltd.

Harris Trust
Tucson, Arizona

Right: *Trust offices.*
Below: *Teller counter.*
Opposite: *Conference room.*
Photography: *Michael Norton.*

Opening the space between the teller line and trust offices to establish a stronger visual relationship was just one of numerous measures by McCarthy Nordburg, Ltd. to renovate and expand a conventional, 25-year-old, 4,710-square foot bank building in the desert foothills of Tucson, Arizona to serve as a branch of Harris Trust for high net worth financial clients. Interestingly, a major constraint in the facility, the existing ceiling structure, helped define the design and create interest throughout the space. An existing duct, for example, was transformed into a sweeping curve that is interrupted by a layered wood plane enhanced with recessed light slots. Overall selections of materials and finishes, including muted floor patterns, fine furnishings, wood trim and earthy colors, maintain the building's integrity and create an appealing, upscale space for upscale customers that has already exceeded Harris Trust's expectations.

McCarthy Nordburg, Ltd.

Meridian Enterprise
Phoenix, Arizona

Left: Reception.
Above: Core area.
Below: Open plan area with canopies.
Photography: Michael Norton.

It's impressive what may wait today's tilt-ups. A Motorola division that develops software engineering for the Semiconductor Components Group, Meridian Enterprise has consolidated various metropolitan Phoenix facilities in a 72,000-square foot, high-bay, one-story, tilt-up industrial building. Scarcely ideal though this type of structure is for offices, the interior design by McCarthy Nordburg, Ltd. demonstrates how a raw, industrial building shell can be a superior workplace for 450 employees. The facility's open plan layout surrounds a central core of training rooms, conference rooms, "touch-down" rooms and support services, and it employs floor-to-ceiling walls, exposed cable trays and ceiling canopies to create separate high-tech neighborhoods that say "cool" rather than "tilt-up."

Meyer Associates, Inc.

227 East Lancaster Avenue
Ardmore
Pennsylvania 19003
610.649.8500
610.649.8509 (Fax)
www.meyer-associates.com
www.cooldiggs.com
info@meyer-associates.com

Meyer Associates, Inc.

De Lage Landen Financial Services, Inc.
Berwyn, Pennsylvania

Above left: *Entrance to executive area.*
Above right: *Marketing group in open plan area.*
Right: *Cafeteria.*
Opposite: *Reception area.*
Photography:
Don Pearse Photographers, Inc.

There's no denying that the wholesale shift to open plan space since the 1970s has let corporate America run its offices with greater flexibility and economy. The benefits are abundantly visible in the handsome new, 220,000 square foot, three-story headquarters for 718 employees of De Lage Landen Financial Services, Inc. in Berwyn, Pennsylvania, designed by Meyer Associates, Inc. New ownership and a new chairman caused the global provider of high-quality asset financing products to reduce the sense of hierarchy. To capture the new spirit and accommodate a 100 percent churn rate, the new design reduces the number of private offices from 150 to 10 and introduces demountable full-height partitions, open plan work stations, raised flooring and other dynamic elements. Even the private offices display an unprecedented openness—being framed by only three walls—so the entire organization is genuinely involved. Yet the new facility also offers such amenities as a fitness center, cafeteria and cafe that employees can appreciate no matter where they're stationed at work.

Meyer Associates, Inc.

Provident Mutual Insurance and Financial Services
Berwyn, Pennsylvania

Lower left: *Executive boardroom.*
Bottom left: *Training room.*
Right: *Executive area.*
Below right: *Training breakout area.*
Photography:
Don Pearse Photographers, Inc.

Provident Mutual Insurance in Berwyn, Pennsylvania began in the 1800s, and wanted to convey the dual impression of its heritage and its involvement in the global economy in a new, 110,000 square foot, two-story headquarters for 463 employees designed by Meyer Associates, Inc. Thus, the company asked the designer for a facility that could accommodate growth and churn as well as update institutional culture. Proving that the whole is greater than the sum of its parts, the new headquarters blends timeless architectural millwork with flexible demountable interior partitions; introduces employees to a rich collection of historic artifacts in the training breakout area; and accents a cost-effective and versatile environment with curved walls and art glass. This vision of the past has a bright future.

Meyer Associates, Inc.

ICON Clinical Research
North Wales, Pennsylvania

Left: *Boardroom.*
Below left: *Interior conference room.*
Below right: *Skylight in general office area.*
Opposite: *Reception area.*
Photography: *Don Pearse Photographers, Inc.*

Suddenly a young organization finds it must grow up. It needs a realistic master plan, cost-effective facilities to accommodate growth, and an interior design that defines its corporate culture. Such were the circumstances when ICON Clinical Research, a provider of clinical research studies and biometric services, commissioned Meyer Associates, Inc. to design its 93,000 square foot headquarters for 420 employees in North Wales, Pennsylvania. Having just gone public with limited capital, new clients pouring in and operations expanding rapidly, ICON relocated into a one-story factory that soon proved its worth. High-growth departments were strategically located for ease of expansion, circulation paths and skylights were dramatically used to enliven space, and an "established" culture was portrayed in high-impact areas. Demonstrating that it's a fast learner, ICON has grown to occupy the entire factory quickly and smoothly.

Meyer Associates, Inc.

US Interactive
King of Prussia, Pennsylvania

Among the unexpected dividends of the new economy is an appreciation of how well architects and interior designers can create exciting work environments with limited budgets and tight schedules, such as the new 24,000 square foot, two-story headquarters for US Interactive in King of Prussia, Pennsylvania, designed by Meyer Associates, Inc. US Interactive, an Internet professional services company focusing on customer management solutions for the communications and financial services industries, was in its pre-IPO phase and depended on a venture capital firm for financing. Every cent had to be justified in developing offices, conference room, multi-purpose room and coffee bar to attract and retain 120 young, talented and Internet-savvy employees. The unmistakable "wow" people express upon visiting US Interactive comes from paint, drywall, carpet, industrial fixtures—and the power of good design.

Above: *Conference room with reception area beyond.*
Right: *Coffee bar.*
Photography: *Don Pearse Photographers, Inc.*

Mojo•Stumer Associates, P.C.

14 Plaza Road
Greenvale
New York 11548
516.625.3344
516.625.3418 (Fax)
www.mojostumer.com

Mojo•Stumer Associates, P.C.

GB Capital
New York, New York

Successful people know that moment. Suddenly, they find themselves thinking that a fine watch, high-performance sports sedan or tailored suit no longer seems unattainable or inappropriate. Status quo no longer seems satisfactory, and they aspire to a new and higher level of experience. Such was the unexpected but fortuitous outcome when GB Capital, a New York money management firm, retained Mojo-Stumer Associates to design its new, 14,000-square foot office for 40 employees. With business flourishing, the two partners of this four-year-old enterprise needed room to increase their trading operations. They took over the premises of two tenants on their floor of a midtown office building for the expansion. The partners knew what they wanted —at least in functional

terms—when they asked Mojo-Stumer to design a facility that would include a formal reception area, three trading rooms, a partners' office, three private offices, a conference room, a computer room, a copy/file room and a small pantry. "We could see that adding desks to our trading room would require lots of space, electricity, air conditioning and cabling," the partners recalled. "Since we wanted to receive our clients in a more formal manner, we also upgraded their accommodations. We wanted the circulation arranged so that they could easily be directed towards the conference room or our office, and away from the trading rooms. In addition, we wanted to look directly into the trading rooms from our seats." Having elected to expand its existing office, the firm endured months of phased construction in which the

Opposite: *Trading room.*
Right: *Conference room entrance.*
Overleaf: *Partners' office.*

Above: Reception area
seating.
Above right: Table
lamp and occasional
table in reception area.

staff moved from place
to place as the work pro-
ceeded. With the com-
pletion of the project,
GB Capital took posses-
sion of a highly functional, flexible and economi-
cal facility. However, the
aesthetics of the work-
place, incorporating fine
hardwood, limestone
and stainless steel ele-
ments, were a revelation.
"We had seen and
approved all the floor
plans, renderings and

samples that Mojo-
Stumer showed us," the
partners noted. "But we
had no idea it would be
so handsome until every-
thing was done. We are
thrilled with our new
office."

Montroy Andersen Design Group, Inc.

432 Park Avenue South
New York
New York 10016
212.481.5900
212.481.7481 (Fax)
www.madgi.com

Montroy Andersen Design Group, Inc.

Active Health Management
New York, New York

Left: *Board room.*
Lower left: *Reception and small conference room.*
Bottom left: *Open plan area.*
Opposite: *Stone and wood feature wall.*
Photography: *Phillip Ennis.*

Sometimes the best way to fit into an attractive existing environment is to alter it as little as possible, even if you're a state-of-the-art, Internet-based medical service. So when Active Health Management commissioned Montroy Andersen Design Group, Inc. to designed its 20,000-square foot, two-story office for 85 employees in New York, it wanted to incorporate the natural light, arched windows and high ceiling heights already there. Accordingly, the new facility uses metal and glass partitions to place private offices, open plan work stations and conference rooms at the perimeter, and pantry, toilets, storage and equipment rooms in the core, and features an exposed ceiling with pendant lighting fixtures and visible ductwork, as well as a stone feature wall to separate staff areas from other functions. Whatever fate awaits its field, Active Health Management has a fit new home to shape its destiny.

**Montroy Andersen
Design Group, Inc.**

Montroy Andersen Design Group, Inc.
New York, New York

Can an interior design be assembled as precisely as a fine watch? For Montroy Andersen Design Group, Inc., this challenge resonated with special meaning not long ago, because the client was the architecture and interior design firm itself. Not only did the firm want to properly house its 19 employees on 3,000 square feet of office space in Manhattan, it sought to build a showcase of materials, furnishings and lighting to illustrate options for its clients' own environments. A three-dimensional module was developed as a standard of reference using tall, narrow steel sculptures signifying man, polished steel panel wall inserts and a bi-axial floor plan. Whether or not clients fully understand the modular theory underpinning the architecture and interior design studio, partners' office, conference room, material library and pantry finished in maple and cherry wood, stainless steel, glass, paint, carpet and an assortment of lighting fixtures, they enjoy its unmistakable ambiance of harmony and order. Relatively small as the space is, the staff members, furnishings and advanced computer equipment take their places like the components of a valued timepiece.

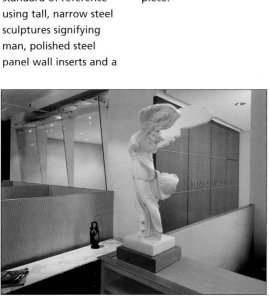

Left: Conference room wall at reception area.
Right: Entry into partners' office.
Above right: Partners' office
Opposite: Design studio.
Photography: Wade Zimmerman.

Montroy Andersen Design Group, Inc.

Fame Information Services
New York, New York

Below left: *Board room.*
Right: *Reception area.*
Below right: *Main perimeter corridor.*
Photography: *Paul Warchol.*

Two streams of people arriving regularly at the 25,000-square foot New York office of Fame Information Services—its own 85 employees plus clients coming for training—could have created recurring headaches for the financial information services firm on its L-shaped floor. However, the design by Montroy Andersen Design Group, Inc., enables the reception area to direct people on their separate ways by planting visual cues that indicate which side contains private offices, open plan work stations areas and a conference area, and which side has training facilities. Defined by a perimeter location and open metal ceiling with spotlights that imitate sunlight, the main employee corridor represents a long walk interrupted half way by an appealing lounge, pantry and mail center. Keeping matters straightforward yet inviting like this gives everyone reasons to look forward to working days here.

Montroy Andersen Design Group, Inc.

USA Networks
New York, New York

Moving with uncommon haste is commonplace in the media and entertainment world, where being second is often akin to being too late. USA Networks, a leading media and entertainment business, knew this when it retained Montroy Andersen Design Group, Inc. to design its 30,000-square foot, three-story corporate headquarters in midtown Manhattan on a fast-track schedule. The design firm responded by serving as architect, interior designer and project manager, preparing to renovate and reuse the previously built installation and negotiating directly with individual subcontractors and suppliers for economy and efficiency. Not only did this strategy result in private offices, open plan areas and conference facilities provided on time and cost, it gave employees access to a landscaped terrace overlooking legendary Central Park and use of a free-flowing and spacious stairway spanning all three levels. Good show!

Montroy Andersen
Design Group, Inc.

Jefferies & Company
Short Hills, New Jersey

Left: Reception area.
Above: Detail of reception desk.
Below left: Trading floor.
Photography: Addisen Thompson.

Adrenaline flows freely in the course of a business day in a trading and securities firm like Jefferies & Company. Markets are linked worldwide, capital crosses borders unchecked, and information travels everywhere instantly, making the financial world volatile and unpredictable. To create an exciting, innovative and up-to-date 18,000-square foot branch office for 90 employees of Jefferies & Company in Short Hills, New Jersey, Montroy Andersen Design Group, Inc. paid close attention to how the company's employees interact, particularly on the critical trading floor at the heart of an environment that includes private and open plan offices, conference rooms, full-service pantry, exercise gym and telecommunications equipment room. Head traders consequently sit on raised floor overlooking wings of trading desks and glass-fronted perimeter offices, leading the conquest of the financial world through good design.

Nelson

The Nelson Building
222-30 Walnut Street
Philadelphia
Pennsylvania 19106
215.925.6562
215.925.9151 (Fax)
www.nelsononline.com
nacorp@nelsononline.com

Atlanta
Baltimore
Chicago
Columbia
Hartford
Jacksonville
Minneapolis
New York
Phoenix
Providence
Richmond
San Francisco
Seattle
Shreveport
St. Louis
Tampa
Wilmington
Winston-Salem

Nelson

Nelson Corporate Headquarters
Philadelphia, Pennsylvania

Below left: *Exterior.*
Right: *Reception.*
Below right: *Executive conference room.*
Bottom right: *Studio.*
Opposite: *Entrance.*
Photography: *Tom Crane.*

Installing a sophisticated 21st century corporate headquarters to manage 19 national locations inside a late 1840s historic brick structure would seem commonplace in Europe. However, the design of the new, 23,000-square foot Philadelphia home office by Nelson, a planning and design firm, for itself is anything but commonplace in America. Besides accommodating five units of the firm's integrated services, including architecture, interior design, workplace services, strategies and information services, in such facilities as corporate offices, studios, library, conference/training center, administrative area, LAN room and call center, the designers have restored and highlighted key elements of the historic building, introducing an exposed network of infrastructure in main work areas, making creative use of existing spaces such as the library in the barrel-vaulted basement, and developing a roof garden so the office's 100 employees can enjoy sweeping vistas of William Penn's city.

CIGNA World Headquarters
Philadelphia, Pennsylvania

Above left:
Boardroom.
Above right: *Staircase.*
Left: *Executive office.*
Opposite: *Interior view from executive office.*
Photography: *Jack Neith.*

Every view from the top is special. Consider the 100,000-square foot, seven-story world headquarters that CIGNA developed for 300 employees atop a new Philadelphia office building. The striking design by Nelson creates an efficient, comfortable and advanced facility for the insurance company that seems effortlessly tailored for the pyramidal shape of the building's uppermost floors. On the other hand, the basic scheme of glass-walled perimeter offices encircling interior workstations succeeds because it carefully accommodates the individual floors' unusual shapes, maze of columns, sloping perime-

ter walls and angled sway braces—which CIGNA wanted exposed. The result is a superior environment of executive offices, corporate offices, conference center, executive dining rooms and full-service kitchen, appointed in fine materials, subtly illuminated and graced with wrap-around views. Donald M. Levinson, executive vice president of CIGNA's human resources and services division, is pleased to note, "We found Nelson able to listen to what we wanted."

Nelson

Bank of America
Northeast Regional Headquarters
Washington, DC

Visitors may never suspect that much of the historic character of the building that houses Bank of America's Northeast Regional Headquarters in Washington, D.C. was lost through repeated alterations. The recent renovation of architectural elements and installation of new MEP infrastructure in the 120,000-square foot, 10-story facility, designed by Nelson for 400 employees, projects such a powerful thematic unity that it's hard to believe the executive offices, corporate offices, conference center and dining rooms are not original. Yet they are the result of extensive research into the building's architecture and comprehensive study of the Bank's needs that guided the reconstruction of the 10 gutted floors. In addition, the use of new and more economical construction materials in place of traditional ones, and a strategic plan that relocated workers to "swing space" without interrupting operations were telling—if invisible—factors in the project's success.

Above left: Reception area.
Above right: Dining room.
Top right: View from elevator lobby.
Opposite: Corridor to executive/conference/dining facilities.
Photography: Tom Crane.

310

Ace Executive Dining Room
Philadelphia, Pennsylvania

Long before anyone could sample the cuisine in the 9,000-square foot Ace Executive Dining Room on the 52nd floor of a Philadelphia office tower, the Nelson design team faced more practical issues. How do you configure the mechanical systems with venting for a full-service kitchen so high up? How do you maximize ceiling heights at the perimeter to exploit the skyline when the walls cant inward? And how do you design an elegant interior without competing against breathtaking views? As the insurance company's executives and their guests will attest, Nelson's solution is delectable.

Above: View towards reception area.
Right: Seating at perimeter.
Photography: Tom Crane.

N2 Design Group Architects, LLP

30 West 26th Street
New York
New York 10010
212.989.7842
212.989.7843 (Fax)
www.n2design.net
harryn@n2design.net

403 Main Street
Suite 3
Port Washington
New York 11050
516.883.4906
516.883.4909 (Fax)

N2 Design Group Architects, LLP

Above: Performance space.
Right: Elevator lobby.
Opposite: Interactive office corridor.
Overleaf: Reception with exposed concrete structure.
Photography: Phillip Ennis.

If you're enjoying the sound of music from artists like Mary J. Blige, Modjo, Patti LaBelle, Lyle Lovett, Chante Moore, Gladys Knight and Semisonic, you're enjoying MCA Records. To create a vital, effective and versatile, 17,500-square foot space for 75 employees of MCA Records befitting a cutting-edge music company, N2 Design Group Architects took a Cubist approach to the walls, ceilings and floors, pro-ducing a composition that opens up the concrete structure, exposes a 19-foot high ceiling, and provides a performance space for 75 people along with offices, conference rooms and lounges. Mary J. Blige, welcome to your music company's office.

N2 Design Group Architects, LLP

ABN-AMRO
Prime Brokerage
New York, New York

Right: A reception area.
Below: Interior stair-case.
Opposite: Conference room.
Photography: Phillip Ennis.

Clients visiting the 55,000 square foot, three-level office of ABN-AMRO Prime Brokerage, a hedge funding and asset management service, may not perceive of the numerous small to medium-size suites that share the reception area, conference rooms, market data rooms, support facilities and pantry. Why? Although the design by N2 Design Group Architects lets suites interpret their own needs individually, the public areas are unified by comprehensive architectural standards that everybody can respect.

N2 Design Group Architects, LLP

Optical Heights
Roslyn Heights, New York

Left: *Entry.*
Right: *Showroom.*
Photography: *Carol Bates*

Start with a narrow and deep storefront in a suburban strip mall, take generous helpings of function and artistry, blend thoroughly and hope you do as well as Optical Heights with its new, 1,200 square foot retail optician's store outfitted with private staff office, lens laboratory, exam room, contact room and showroom in Roslyn Heights, New York. N2 Design Group Architects introduced an urban, SoHo gallery-like ambience, with eyewear displayed adjacent to artwork, on a canvas of angled and curved white walls, wood cabinetry, exposed ceilings, sophisticated lighting and slate and carpet flooring. To encourage touching and feeling of the tangible art, the eyewear is not displayed behind glass showcases. Shoppers will enjoy their visual experience.

O'Brien Travis Jaccard Inc.

1825 Connecticut Avenue, NW
Suite 300
Washington, DC 20009
202.939.0300
202.234.2900 (Fax)
www.otjinc.com
info@otjinc.com

O'Brien Travis Jaccard Inc.

O'Brien Travis Jaccard Inc.
Washington, D.C.

Does good design pay? Just 12 months after the architecture firm of O'Brien Travis Jaccard Inc. moved its 13 employees into a 5,700-square foot office in Washington, D.C., it has filled the space to capacity at 25 employees. If there is a lesson to be drawn from the design of the reception, conference room, partners' offices, studio, design library, and team work/lunchroom area, it might be that good design can pay very handsomely. On a more practical level, good design enabled the firm to turn a building shell compromised by a low, 8-foot, 6-inch, slab-to-slab height and "bowling alley" corridors into an airy, open and exciting workplace that shows clients a wide range of construction materials and methods. This includes various wood species and paint finishes, different ways to mount doors, numerous lighting fixtures and more. At the very least, these architects practice what they preach.

Above: Reception area.
Below left: Team/lunch area.
Below right: Studio with library beyond.

Opposite: Conference room with team/lunch area beyond.
Photography: Thomas Arledge.

O'Brien Travis Jaccard Inc.

American Legacy Foundation
Washington, D.C.

Although the incidence of smoking among American teenagers may be running counter to comparable statistics the Federal and state governments have gone on record to oppose the habit. In fact, the American Legacy Foundation was established in Washington, D.C. to reduce tobacco usage among all ages as part of the $206 billion tobacco settlement in November 1996. A 20,000-square foot facility has been designed by O'Brien Travis Jaccard Inc. to house its 75 employees. The office is designed to aid the Foundation in defining its image, accommodating its mission and appealing to employees and the public. What makes the design solution particularly interesting is the skill it brings to fulfilling the Foundation's three goals: to reduce youth tobacco use, lower exposure to second-hand smoke, and raise the quit rate. Creating a well balanced facility that is forward-thinking, as shown in the caucus rooms; inspiring, as shown in the two "rotundas" that display current activities; and sophisticated, such as the executive offices and conference area; the Foundation is well prepare to fulfill its important mission.

Left: Main reception.
Lower left: Caucus room.
Right: Corridor in "Truth" rotunda.
Lower right: Boardroom.
Opposite: Reception beyond "American Legacy" rotunda.
Photography: Max Mackenzie.

O'Brien Travis Jaccard Inc.   Westfield Realty Inc.
Arlington, Virginia

Above: *Connecting staircase.*
Right: *Private office with downtown view.*
Below: *Private office with lounge seating.*
Opposite: *Reception area on lower level.*
Photography: *Max Mackenzie.*

Wait a minute. The name outside proclaims Westfield Realty. Yet the interior resembles an art gallery. It's not by accident that Westfield Realty, a real estate developer, property manager and contractor, commissioned O'Brien Travis Jaccard Inc. to design a 21,000-square foot, two-level office in Arlington, Virginia to display works of contemporary art. The three founders of Westfield Realty and their three sons (by birth and by marriage) deliberately set out to create a functional, adaptable and cost-effective workplace for a staff of 45 whose reception areas, private offices, conference rooms, general office areas, galleries and lunchrooms would all be suitable backdrops for their art collection. In addition, they wanted to take advantage of the spectacular views of downtown Washington and to create separate "senior" and "junior" suites, reflecting their individual personalities, within a harmonious

overall design. Out of these program requirements has emerged an office design of sweeping curves and angular intersections that respond to the building's distinctive shape, while simultaneously creating a fine place for doing business and a fine place for showing art. Why should it be anything less?

Above: Junior suite reception area.
Right: View from junior suite reception into private office.

OP·X

21 Dupont Circle, NW
Washington DC 20036
202.822.9797
202.785.0443 (Fax)
www.opxglobal.com
info@opxglobal.com

OP·X

WorldSpace, Inc. Washington, D.C. and London, U.K.

Left: World headquarters lobby.
Lower left: *ROC satellite operations facility.*
Lower right: *World headquarters staircase.*
Photography: *Alan Karchmer.*

WorldSpace could emerge as a leader in satellite broadcasting if a new medium, the direct digital broadcast of entertainment and information via radio, is used by sizable audiences equipped with newly developed handheld receivers in Africa, Asia and South and Central America. Success will enable the company to attain at least one of two major goals: being a profitable business and fulfilling a social mission in providing media to underserved populations in these three continents. Impressive examples of its resolve can be seen in new facilities in Washington, D.C. and London, U.K., designed by OP·X, in coordination with Spence Harris Hogan. Significantly, WorldSpace has located its 86,000-square foot world headquarters and first regional operations center (ROC) in the nation's capital, at 2400 N Street, N.W., the former home of U.S. News & World Report, even though most high-technology businesses in the Potomac region reside in Virginia and Maryland. Its sleek, modern headquarters feature a two-story entrance lobby, glass conference rooms and video conferencing in the Summit and Presentation Rooms. Handsome as this space is, its requirements pale before those of the 11,000-square foot Regional Operations Center. The ROC is a 24/7 facility that enables the AfriStar satellite to broadcast programming to Africa from a geostationary orbit 22,000 miles above earth.

Above: *World headquarters Presentation Room.*

Right: European head-
quarters atrium and
media wall.
Photography: Tim
Soar.

Above: European headquarters conference room in historic structure.

Below: European headquarters media center.

The function is partly accomplished through extensive infrastructure installed on premises, including separate and redundant mechanical and electrical systems, raised flooring, advanced environmental controls, ergonomic office design and—since the mission-critical facility is also a showcase for clients and guests—a visitor's gallery. For uplinks to the AfriStar satellite, WorldSpace has also developed a 25,000-square foot European headquarters and beam technical facility in London's media district, at 4-6 Soho Square, that uplinks content to the satellite for broadcast. Though Africans will be more concerned about the quality of WorldSpace programming, the London facility is both a superb place to work as well as a potent symbol in Europe, an historic, timber-framed structure that now houses three ground-floor, on-air studios, satellite uplink, offices and reception focused on a two-story atrium. A new era in satellite broadcasting is off to a rousing start.

333

OP·X

Net 2000
Communications
Herndon, Virginia

Top: *Boardroom.*
Above: *Lobby.*
Left: *Closing room.*
Photography:
*Hoachlander Davis
Photography.*

Ready, set, go! Like a time bomb placed on the doorstep by a competitor, the need to abridge time-to-market has accelerated high-tech facility development. Net 2000 Communications, a high-tech start-up, hired OP-X to design its 126,000-square foot, three-level office for 450 employees in Herndon, Virginia, when its payroll doubled in four months. Yet the company transcended sheer numbers by deciding that this project was not just about cost effectiveness in creating a network operations center, customer response center and switch, but also about quality conditions for employees. Thus, there are abundant teaming areas, conference rooms and quiet rooms balancing open plan areas, good natural and indirect lighting, and a 1:200 density supporting a very happy staff.

OP·X

Hunton & Williams
Washington, D.C.

Right: *Skylighted reception area.*
Below: *Secretarial office area.*
Photography: *Alan Karchmer.*

Conservative as the practice of law has remained over the centuries, the swift rise of technology, the global economy and communication and transportation networks is steadily transforming it nonetheless. For example, keeping abreast of dynamic personnel and technology requirements has visibly shaped the new 110,000-square foot law offices of Hunton & Williams in Washington, D.C., designed by OP·X. The development of an interior including a reception area, private offices, conference center, support services and a wellness center has centered on the creation of a perimeter office partitioning system for reconfiguring without affecting doors and clerestories, and a support layout that can adapt without physical modification, all appointed in a design that displays the timeless materials and craftsmanship that Washington expects in law offices.

1120 19th Street
Washington, D.C.

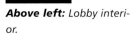

Above left: *Lobby interior.*
Above right: *Exterior canopy.*
Photography: *Maxwell Mackenzie.*

People who don't judge books by their covers haven't read much lately, and savvy commercial property owners who can exploit the growing role of design in modern life are updating their lobbies to project a trendy welcome to tenants and visitors alike. Thus, real estate developer and property manager JBG asked OP·X to renovate the lobby of 1120 19th Street in downtown Washington —but with a twist. OP·X's makeover could not alter existing dimensions or touch in-situ travertine and other existing finishes. Making a virtue of necessity, OP·X has exploited a static ceiling and ordinary facade by introducing an articulated soffit overhead that adds a sense of forward movement, and a glass facade topped by a canopy to project a fresh, signature appearance on the street.

Oliver Design Group

One Park Plaza
Cleveland
Ohio 44114
216.696.7300
216.696.5834 (Fax)
www.odgarch.com

Oliver Design Group

The Hammer Company Headquarters
Cleveland, Ohio

Left: *Wine tasting room.*
Above: *Wine cellar.*
Below: *Corridor.*
Opposite: *Great Hall.*
Photography: *Dan Cunningham.*

An established, family-owned wine importer and wholesaler, The Hammer Company of Cleveland wanted more than a standard headquarters for its 50 employees, so Oliver Design Group designed a 18,000 square foot facility like no other. Two requirements shaped it decisively: creating a Tudor-style environment on a limited budget, and combining entertainment and marketing activities with business operations. While the facility has executive offices, general offices, support areas and a board room as other organizations do, it also features a wine tasting room, wine cellar, gourmet kitchen and auditorium. An inspired design with real and faux materials and a Great Hall that keeps marketing and operations separate but close make everything work. Says G. Daniel Hammer, "We are extremely proud of our new offices."

Oliver Design Group

Ohio Savings Plaza and Park Plaza
Public Spaces
Cleveland, Ohio

Left: *Ohio Savings Plaza.*
Opposite: *Elevator lobby.*
Lower left: *Guard's desk at Ohio Savings Plaza.*
Photography: *Dan Cunningham.*

First time. First job. First date. First impressions do matter in corporate real estate, and few spaces offer as good an opportunity to make good first impressions as building lobbies. Thus, the owner of two multi-tenant office buildings in the heart of Cleveland's financial district, Ohio Savings Plaza and Park Plaza, retained Oliver Design Group to create an elegant series of lobbies and common areas to attract new tenants in a competitive market. Working with a modest budget, the designers re-used existing elements wherever possible, introduced new, elements as needed, and redesigned the surfaces and lighting. Notes David Goldberg, senior vice president, Ohio Savings Bank, "Our lobbies are now contemporary, solid and elegant. Oliver exactly hit the mark."

Oliver Design Group

Eaton Corporation World Headquarters
Cleveland, Ohio

Left: *Corridor.*
Below: *Glass interior office wall.*
Opposite: *Entrance to conference room.*
Photography: *Dan Cunningham.*

In a quiet yet profound change, Eaton Corporation, a Fortune 500 automotive engine components manufacturer, has embraced new office design standards for its world headquarters in Cleveland that are based not so much on hierarchy, its traditional criterion, as on the more open and egalitarian basis of job task. Evidence of this change can already be seen in the new interiors created by Oliver Design Group. Within the executive offices, for example, private offices have transparent and translucent glass interior office walls to preserve privacy yet foster accessibility. Private

offices in general are smaller with translucent glass, while managers and directors occupy open plan work stations that use glass similarly. As for the new training center, it is as flexible as possible to accommodate various types of sessions and sizes of groups, and provides breakout areas equipped with mobile furnishings. A new era has begun auspiciously at Eaton.

Oliver Design Group

The Technology Learning Center
Cuyahoga Community College
Cleveland, Ohio

Above left: *Exterior.*
Above right: *Electronic work stations.*
Photography: *Al Teufen.*

Time will tell whether the Internet and other information technologies will turn many college students into long-distance learners. For now, the Technology Learning Center, a new, 35,000-square foot facility designed by Oliver Design Group for Cleveland's Cuyahoga Community College, stands as a bold, early attempt to explore the spatial demands for educating 250 students and business people using the latest technology tools in six electronic classrooms, and equipping 150 electronic work stations for independent, technology-assisted learning by students and faculty. Occupying a gutted lecture hall annex, the Center facilitates student interaction and visual control by staff, giving cyberspace friendly, human features.

Perkins & Will

800.837.9455
gary.wheeler@perkinswill.com
www.perkinswill.com

Atlanta
Charlotte
Chicago
Los Angeles
Miami
Minneapolis
New York
Paris

DiamondCluster International
Chicago, Illinois

Above left: *Open plan area.*
Above right: *Digital lobby.*
Photography:
Christopher Barrett/ Hedrich Blessing.

At first, anyone seriously involved in electronic business or "e-business" seemed to be a T-shirt-and-jeans-clad twentysomething, clocking 24/7 hours in a warehouse. Now, corporate America is discovering the potential of e-business for improving the speed, accuracy, breadth and profitability of business-to-business transactions. Consider Diamond Cluster International, an e-business strategic con-sulting firm that retained Perkins & Will to design a 60,000-square foot, two-level office in Chicago for 300 people. The young firm is growing rapidly, yet it requested a substantial, CEO-level environment in a compressed time frame that was cost-effective, multi-functional and team-oriented. No wonder visitors are impressed when they see the reception area, dedicated work offices, teaming spaces, training facility, digital lobby and IT support environment designed in a classic, International Style using birdseye maple, ebonized wood, granite, lacquer, stainless steel and glass. The kids are growing up.

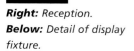

Right: Reception.
Below: Detail of display fixture.

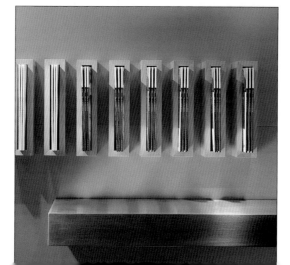

Perkins & Will

The Goodrich Company
Charlotte, North Carolina

Right: Three-story atrium.
Below: Executive office.
Photography: Christopher Barrett/ Hedrich Blessing.

Children aren't the only people wondering what adults actually do for a living. Due to the increasingly complex, multi-disciplinary and collaborative nature of work, even employees of the same company may have no idea how their colleagues contribute to the finished product.

Thus, the design of a 115,000-square foot *headquarters for the aerospace, performance materials and engineered industrial products division* for Goodrich in Charlotte, North Carolina, by Perkins & Will was unusual from the start. Goodrich identified such conventional

requirements as executive offices, general office areas, boardroom, conference center, training room, video conferencing facility, computer/ server room and cafeteria. However, the company wanted its three main floors to be connected so employees could view its activities. The solution: a

polished, modern office with a three-story atrium where all conference, video conference and training facilities are grouped. Notes David Burner, CEO of Goodrich, "The accolades reverberate from our new home in Charlotte."

Above: Boardroom with sculpture from Goodrich Art Collection.
Right: Atrium stairway seen through conference room.

Perkins & Will

American Hospital Association
Chicago, Illinois

How do you divide a space three ways without leaving unsightly edges? The American Hospital Association faced this situation in constructing a 42,000-square foot, two-level facility in Chicago, designed by Perkins & Will, for 175 employees of three for-profit subsidiaries. Each subsidiary would share the reception area, yet be free to develop its own office design. To empower the subsidiaries, the design team has introduced a clean and graceful modern interior employing an aluminum stickwall system for framing spaces with full-height glass walls and doors that can be reconfigured as the need arises. Existing pendant light fixtures provide indirect, computer-friendly lighting for an environment that includes open and private offices, boardroom, collaborative work spaces, teaming areas, heads-down meeting spaces and hoteled offices, all served by a single reception area. Far from looking compromised, the facility has won honors.

Above: General office area.
Top: Reception.
Right: Meeting space.
Opposite: Collaborative work area.
Photography: Christopher Barrett/ Hedrich Blessing.

Perkins & Will

**Swiss Re America
U.S. Headquarters
North Castle, New York**

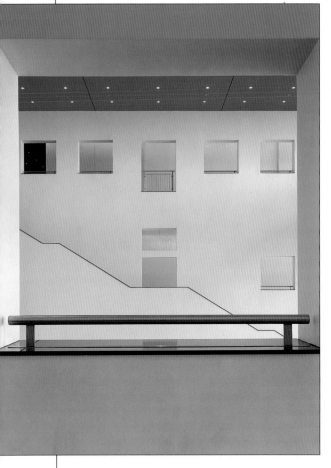

Left: Entry stair hall.
Above right: *Dining.*
*Below left: General
office area.*
Photography: *Eduard
Hueber/Arch Photo, Inc.*

Like aircraft carriers, large offices operate differently from their smaller counterparts. To design Swiss Re America's U.S. headquarters on 320,000 square feet in a new, three-story building in North Castle, New York, Perkins & Will, *in association with Iu & Biblowicz,* had to account for the well-being of personnel and flexibility for reconfiguration on a vast scale. Work spaces are standardized on three modular types and equipped with ergonomic seating. Quality lighting is supplemented by ample daylight. Power, voice and data systems are distributed under 6-inch raised flooring for easy access. Along with such amenities as training rooms, dining areas and a fitness center, there are privacy rooms for use by staff to make the reinsurance company's facility as good as it is large.

Perkins Eastman Architects PC

115 Fifth Avenue
New York
New York 10003
212.353.7200   Charlotte
212.353.7676 (Fax)   Pittsburgh
www.peapc.com   Stamford
info@peapc.com   Toronto

Perkins Eastman Architects PC   Mount Sinai/NYU Health
Executive Offices
New York, New York

Providing quality health care at reasonable cost has challenged the health care community for years, but one of the benefits from this tumultuous era has been recognition of design's role in enhancing therapeutic outcomes. As a leading hospital and health care management organization, Mount Sinai/NYU Health has employed design with skill and economy in developing its 12,400-square foot executive offices in New York for 21 employees with Perkins Eastman Architects PC. To combine the executive office suite and conference center in a long, narrow building with a continuous skylight on its north facade, the architect has created a central administrative and circulation spine with conference rooms on the north side and executive offices on the south. Combining basic building materials with anigre wood panels and comfortable furnishings creates a warm, inviting setting that reflects what today's consumers want from health care.

Left: *Reception.*
Above: *Board room.*
Below: *Central administrative and circulation spine.*
Photography: *Chuck Choi.*

Perkins Eastman Architects PC

Consumers Union
Yonkers, New York

A trusted evaluator of the nation's consumer products, Consumers Union has exercised the same diligence in developing its corporate headquarters and testing facility in Yonkers, New York, that it does in testing everything from diapers to sport utility vehicles. Indeed, visitors to the 241,000-square foot facility for 600 employees, representing a 171,000-square foot renovation and a 70,000-square foot addition designed by Perkins Eastman Architects PC, find themselves in a pragmatic environment that also happens to be attractive and pleasant. The facility's design is driven by the organization's mission. Each design decision, for example, is a "Best Buy," with everything considered to optimize the use of the budget. An industrial design vocabulary prevails not only because of its appropriateness, but also its minimal cost; and ecological and energy issues are addressed wherever possible. Details like these assure the nation that Consumers Union follows its own advice.

Above left: Testing department atrium.
Above right: Ramp to cafeteria.
Right: Cafeteria.
Left: West wing atrium stairs.
Opposite: West wing atrium.
Photography: Chuck Choi.

Perkins Eastman Architects PC   HealthMarket Incorporated
Norwalk, Connecticut

Right: Mezzanine cat-walk bridge to "fish bowl" conference room.
Below left: The "Park" and bar.
Below right: Private offices.
Opposite: Corridor to board room.
Photography: Addison Thompson.

Working at Internet speed is normal for HealthMarket Incorporated, a Web-based health service in Norwalk, Connecticut. So asking Perkins Eastman Architects PC for a 54,000-square foot renovation in six months may not have seemed unusual. However, the rapid creation of a workplace for 210 employees featuring private offices and open plan work stations, conference rooms, teaming areas, lounges and a full-service kitchen required a close working relationship among the architect, client, con-struction manager and vendors. Communication occurred at all hours of the day and night, and company executives took part in developing a sensitive workplace for the rapidly growing staff. As a result, the open-plan environment of cedar and heavy gauge steel has not elicited a single complaint from a staff that numbered just eight at the time the design was approved.

Perkins Eastman Architects PC   American Financial Group
New York, New York

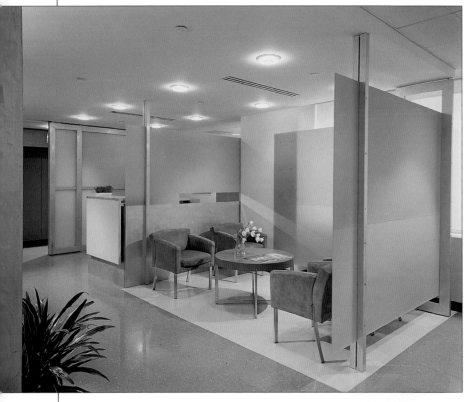

How do you build a sophisticated and memorable image to attract discerning e-commerce clients on a tight budget and timetable? When American Financial Group, an e-commerce business, retained Perkins Eastman Architects PC to design a 14,230-square foot office in New York City for 56 employees, its desire for a new facility that expressed openness and freshness was satisfied by novel spatial configurations in public areas using such basic materials as acrylic panels, Venetian stucco, aluminum structural members and stone. The distinguishing feature of the interior design is the dynamic arrangement of floating walls, suspended between the floor and the ceiling, rather than full-height partitions, which are restricted to areas requiring acoustic privacy and security. Simple complexity or complex simplicity—it works.

Preston T. Phillips Architect

P.O. Box 3037
Bridgehampton
New York 11932
631.537.1237
631.537.5071 (Fax)
www.prestontphillips.com
ptparch@aol.com

Preston T. Phillips
Architect

The J. Jill Group
Corporate Headquarters
Quincy, Massachusetts

Left: View across entrance atrium to reception desk.
Lower left: Executive office with private conference area.
Above: Board room with matched table and ceiling recess; specially commissioned artwork to blend with tone of interiors.
Opposite: Lower floor reception below atrium bridge.
Photography: Peter Aaron/Esto.

What do women want? In the women's apparel market, a major challenge has been to develop a distinctive position between classic, timeless styling and fashion-forward trendiness to please women in their working years. One of the most successful contenders is the J. Jill Group, a catalogue merchant with a retail store presence, for which Preston T. Phillips Architect has designed key facilities, including its headquarters, distribution and fulfillment center and retail stores. The 72,000-square foot, two-story headquarters in Quincy, Massachusetts for 140 employees typifies the close attention given to J. Jill's requirements, which include reception, conference and board rooms, executive offices, design labs, work rooms, projection rooms, break areas and open-plan work spaces. Since the fashion house's many functions require their

own, specific working conditions, the design encompasses a wide range of physical environments that range from the loft-like work rooms, displaying exposed building systems, to the highly finished central atrium, executive offices and conference facilities, which are finely appointed—all under the J. Jill brand. Like any expert tailor, J. Jill appreciates the craftsmanship. Says Gordon R. Cooke, CEO, "I asked Preston (Phillips) to create working and retail environments in keeping with the J. Jill concepts of function, uniqueness and attention to detail. He has delivered for us again and again." Customer satisfaction is as good for architecture as it is for fashion.

Below: *Creative and film areas with tackable curved wall.*

Top right: *Passageway showing example of art collection outside Boardroom.*
Top left: *Break room, one of numerous employee amenities.*
Above: *Design work room showing exposed building elements.*

365

Preston T. Phillips Architect

The J. Jill Group
Distribution Center
Tilton, New Hampshire

As many dot-coms have belatedly discovered, distribution and fulfillment are "old economy" skills that any business must master to sell products by catalogue, telephone or Internet. The J. Jill Group, a women's clothier with a substantial catalogue business and a growing retail operation, was well aware of this in retaining Preston T. Phillips Architect to design a state-of-the-art distribution and fulfillment center for 350 employees in Tilton, New Hampshire. The architect designed a reception building with cafeteria and fitness center, 90,000-square foot administration building with private offices, open-plan office areas, conference facilities, a 12,000-square foot call center for 24/7 operations, all servicing a 400,000-square foot distribution center on 120 acres. To ensure the center's success, the apparel house cooperated closely with the architect to develop optimum working environments featuring natural light and views as well as numerous amenities that suit employees almost as well as J. Jill clothes.

Above left: Partial view of call center.
Above right: Second floor open work stations with a view into central atrium.
Right: Fitness center above cafeteria.
Below right: Cafeteria with exposed elements and roof dormers.
Below: View of dining terrace at dusk showing reception building between the administration building (left) and corner of distribution facility (right).
Opposite: Staircase featuring a neon sculpture.
Photography: Bruce T. Martin.

Preston T. Phillips Architect

The J. Jill Group
Retail Store
Portland, Oregon

What would it be like if consumers could step inside their favorite catalogues? This was the goal for The J. Jill Group in commissioning Preston T. Phillips Architect to develop a prototype retail store for this leading direct mail purveyor of women's clothing. To create a three-dimensional counterpart to J. Jill's catalogue photography, depicting young women alone or with young children at home or in natural landscapes, the architect has established a sequence of spaces dressed in fabrics, stone, plaster, bleached wood and satin nickel to take customers from an inviting storefront and recessed, draped entrance vestibule, where the sound of falling water is heard from the adjacent accessories room, to the main selling area, its curved feature wall and the fitting rooms behind. Welcome home, J. Jill customer.

Richard Pollack & Associates

214 Grant Avenue
Suite 450
San Francisco
California 94108
415.788.4400
415.788.5309 (Fax)
www.RPAarch.com

Richard Pollack & Associates

The Hamel Group
Oakland, California

Before the dot.com movement pushed progressive workspaces into the forefront of design, The Hamel Group trusted RPA's impressions and saw an opportunity to do something different. As an employment marketing firm specializing in the biotech industry, they needed to be credible to the technology world and inviting to the employees who populate it. The central design element (and key to the project's success) gives a complex impression of being stretched and surrounded at the same time, while its texture mirrors the experience of coming into the space from the outside world -rough to smooth. This form, enhanced with ambient lighting is undeniably modern, yet interactive. Since the public and private work environment moves around and through the omnipresent shape to navigate through the space, there's a strong sense of connection and place. Multilayered. Secure. Fluid. The Hamel space is a perfect balance of science and art.

Above left: *Custom reception desk.*
Above: *Conference facilities are folded into the core space.*
Opposite: *The public core is contained in a freeform sculpture.*
Photography: *Jon Miller/Hedrich Blessing.*

Richard Pollack & Associates

Nonstop Solutions
San Francisco, California

Right: *A café occupies the center of the floor plan.*
Photography: *Jon Miller/Hedrich Blessing.*

When Nonstop Solutions decided to consolidate their corporate offices into a 25,000 s.f. space shaped like an E, RPA planned each finger of the E shape as a container for the company's three main work groups and located common areas in the center, thus allowing these diverse groups to interact and feel like one team. The project also features a unique oval metallic ceiling detail that both links the spaces and draws them together. A central cafe connected to the lobby provides a social atmosphere and impromptu workstations, and the furnishings selected throughout the project allow for endless reconfiguration and expansion. The building's E shape was especially beneficial for natural light, with the majority of workspaces enjoying a window seat. Nonstop's solution was simple: Design that uses existing structure to an advantage, and creates the right environment for today's dynamic businesses—fun, functional. flexible.

Left: Meeting spaces dot the open-plan landscape.
Above: High-tech meets warehouse in reception.

Richard Pollack & Associates

Charles Schwab Denver Call & Data Center
Denver, Colorado

When you dial an 800 area code number of an organization whose "operators are standing by," you are answered by someone in a call center, essentially a human warehouse for processing telephone orders that is staffed by hundreds of telemarketers. Working conditions within early call and data centers left much to be desired, but progressive employers have strived to enhance the call center environment. At Charles Schwab Denver Call & Data Center, Denver, Colorado, designed by Richard Pollack & Associates, the 4-story, 150,000-square foot structure provides facilities for work, training, meals and relaxation that incorporate attractive, contemporary furniture, better-grade finishes, sophisticated lighting, bright colors and state-of-the-art building systems to keep some 1000 employees comfortably at work. Brokerage customers of Charles Schwab & Co. may never know where its call center operators spend their working hours. However, they will certainly enjoy the superior service.

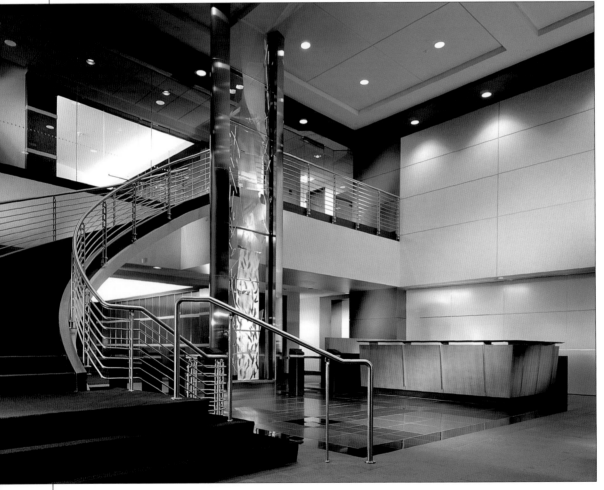

Above: Glass art portrays the facility as information conduit.
Top: Long vistas are deliberately interrupted to add intimacy.
Opposite: Enclosed spaces modulate large, open floor areas.
Photography: Chris Barrett/Hedrich Blessing.

Richard Pollack & Associates

Productopia
San Francisco, California

Dot.coms and other Internet-related businesses have tested the capabilities of architects and interior designers with nanosecond schedules, tight budgets and unpredictable space and manpower needs. Yet the commotion can result in excellent workplaces, as can be seen at Productopia, San Francisco, designed by Richard Pollack & Associates. Productopia is a now-defunct Internet provider of "unbiased product advice" on top consumer products in dozens of merchandise categories. They wanted to develop a serviceable setting that could be eventually upgraded with distinguished furniture, office products and graphics. A handsome, 15,840-square foot interior for 100 employees highlighted by dramatic, axial ceiling planes and rich colors gave the fledgling, pre-IPO company a dynamic, cost-effective and scalable environment where the sky seemed the limit.

Above: *Classic George Nelson lighting accents the conference room.*
Left: *Floating ceiling and wall planes define reception.*
Photography: *Sharon Risedorph, Sharon Risedorph Photography.*

RMW architecture & interiors

160 Pine Street
San Francisco
California 94111
415.781.9800
415.788.5216 (Fax)
info.rmw.com

40 South Market Street
4th Floor
San Jose
California 95113
408.294.8000
408.294.1747 (Fax)

555 Fifth Street
Suite 200
Santa Rosa
California 95401
707.573.0715
707.573.3056 (Fax)

1718 Third Street
Suite 101
Sacramento
California 95814
916.449.1400
916.449.1414 (Fax)

2601 Blake Street
Suite 400
Denver
Colorado 80205
303.297.2400
303.296.0122 (Fax)

www.rmw.com

Phenomenal as the rise of the computer hardware and software industry has been in northern California's Silicon Valley, other forms of economic life can and do thrive there. In fact, KnightRidder, America's second largest newspaper company, recently relocated its headquarters from Miami, Florida, to a handsome, two-story, 40,000-square foot space designed by RMW architecture & interiors in San Jose's Fairmont Plaza, a prestigious downtown office tower. Why did the publisher of 31 newspapers and 33 associated Web sites that generate $2.9 billion in annual revenue become Silicon Valley's 14th largest publicly-held business and 14th Fortune 500 company? The ironic answer: Location. People prize physical proximity to other people even in the Internet age.

Right: Circular forms are utilized in the reception area to frame the view overlook Silicon Valley in KnightRidder's new headquarters.
Photography: Scott McDonald/Hedrich Blessing© 1999

Below: The boardroom blends state-of-the-art information technology and sleek, contemporary interior design.
Right: Corridors are flooded with natural light transmitted through glass and hardwood partitions enclosing private offices.

Below left: A dining facility and lounge area provide flexibility for various corporate functions.

Below: Various meeting areas large and small are provided to accommodate a wide range of visitors and activities.

KnightRidder wanted no less by charging its design firm to fulfill two primary objectives: 1) establish KnightRidder's presence at the heart of the high-tech community, and 2) create a sophisticated and comfortable work environment to take advantage of commanding views and natural light. The design solution does no less by placing employees in an airy, spacious and dynamic setting where private offices occupy each floor's perimeter, open plan offices, support and common areas fill the interior, and a neutral color scheme acts as a backdrop for rich, figured woods, stone, terrazzo, brushed metal and patterned glass. Will KnightRidder find its place within the Valley's unique, entrepreneurial culture? Its splendid new home gives it a head start.

INDEX BY PROJECTS